EASY DUETS for UKULELE

Ondřej Šárek

Spruce Solid Top Soprano Ukulele and LU Series Tenor Ukulele cover image courtesy of Lanikai Ukuleles.

I0806956

WWW.MELBAY.COM

Contents

Introduction

This book contains 30 songs arranged for two ukulele players. The tunes come from different musical genres, including American gospel and folk songs, Christmas carols and classical selections. The collection is good for beginners who don't want to play alone, as well as for slightly more advanced players who want to foster an interest in the ukulele in someone else.

About Performing This Music

In these arrangements, the first ukulele player always plays the melody, sometimes adding a second voice or harmony— but all within the first three frets. As Ukulele 1 is playing the lead, it is necessary to play slightly louder than Ukulele 2, who only plays on open strings. Naturally, the Ukulele 2 part is suitable for all beginners. In this part, however, it is essential to observe the duration of notes, occasionally muting a tone with the left or right hand; otherwise, unwanted dissonances may occur.

How to Read Tablature

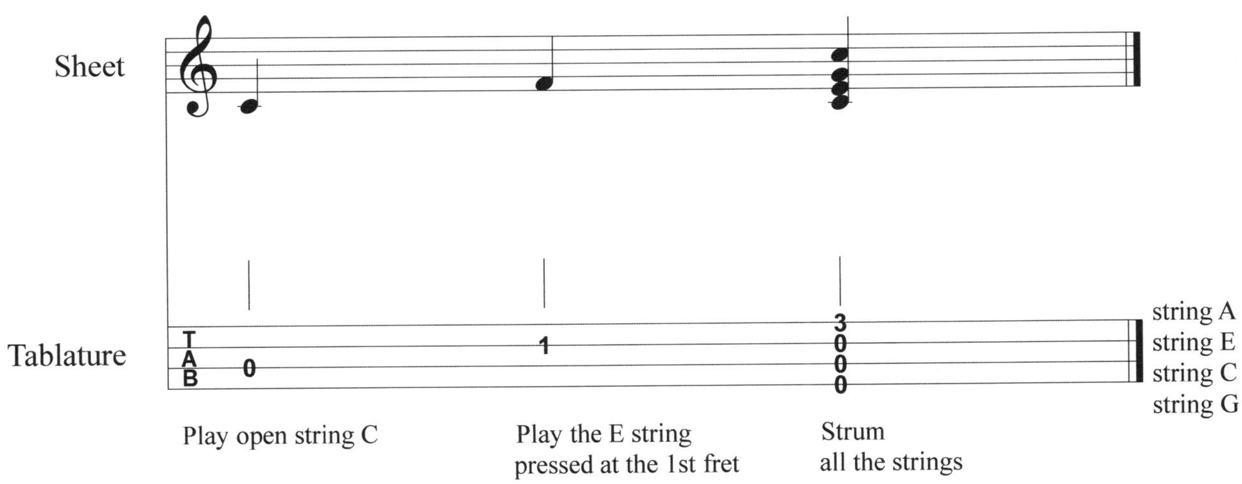

Bile Them Cabbage Down

American Old-Time

arr: Ondřej Šárek

Can Can

Jacques Offenbach (1819-1880)

arr: Ondřej Šárek

Drink It Down

American folk song
arr: Ondřej Šárek

I Saw Three Ships

English carol

arr: Ondřej Šárek

Michael, Row the Boat Ashore

Gospel

arr: Ondřej Šárek

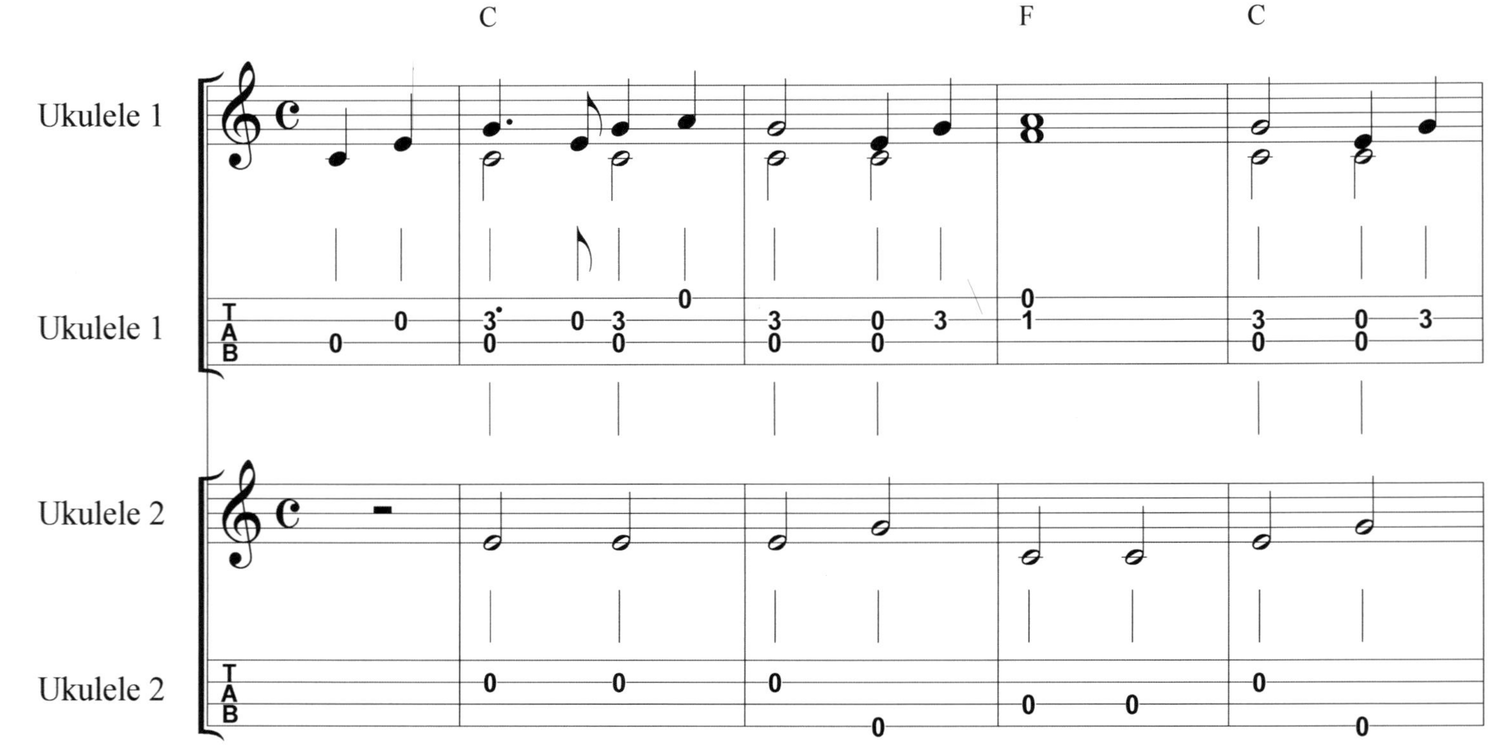

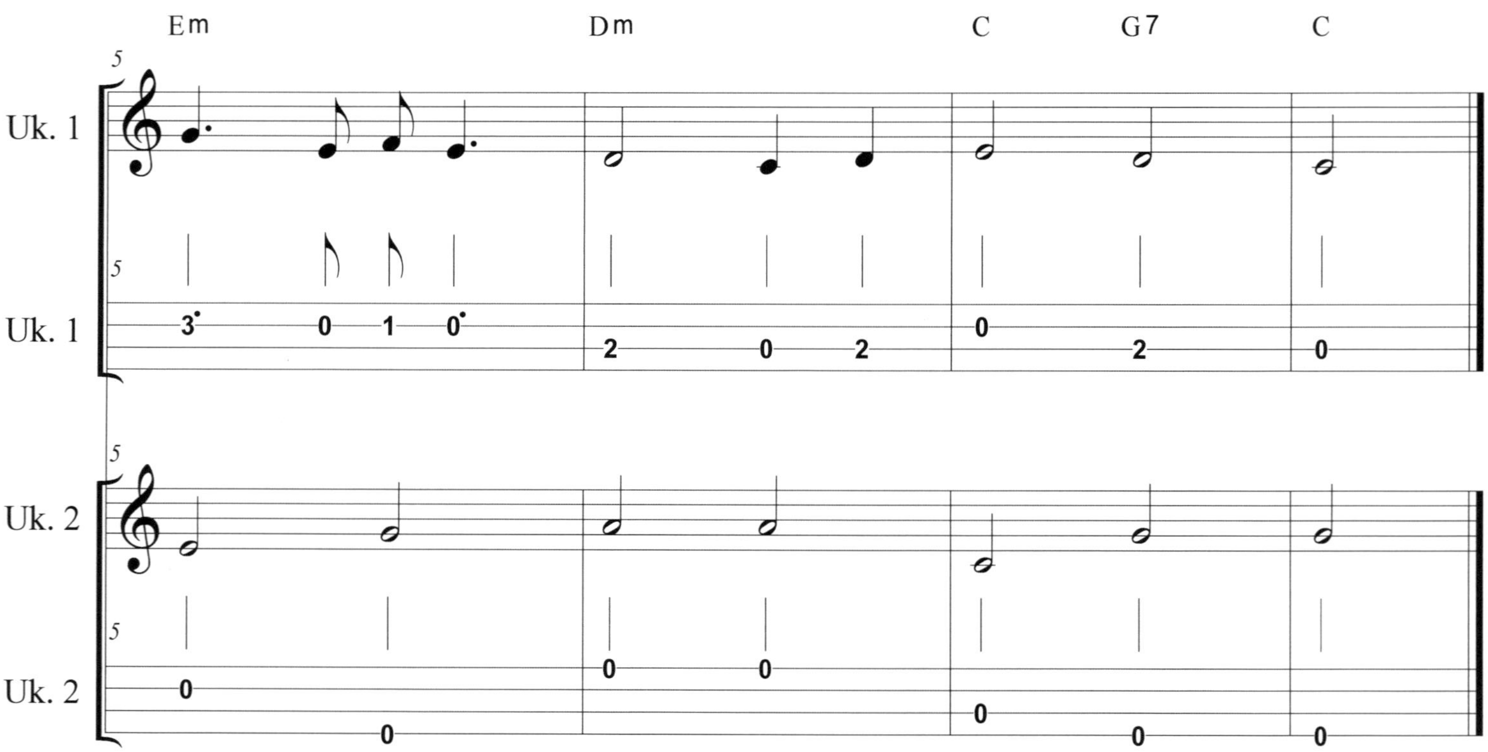

Oh, My Darling Clementine

American folk song
arr: Ondřej Šárek

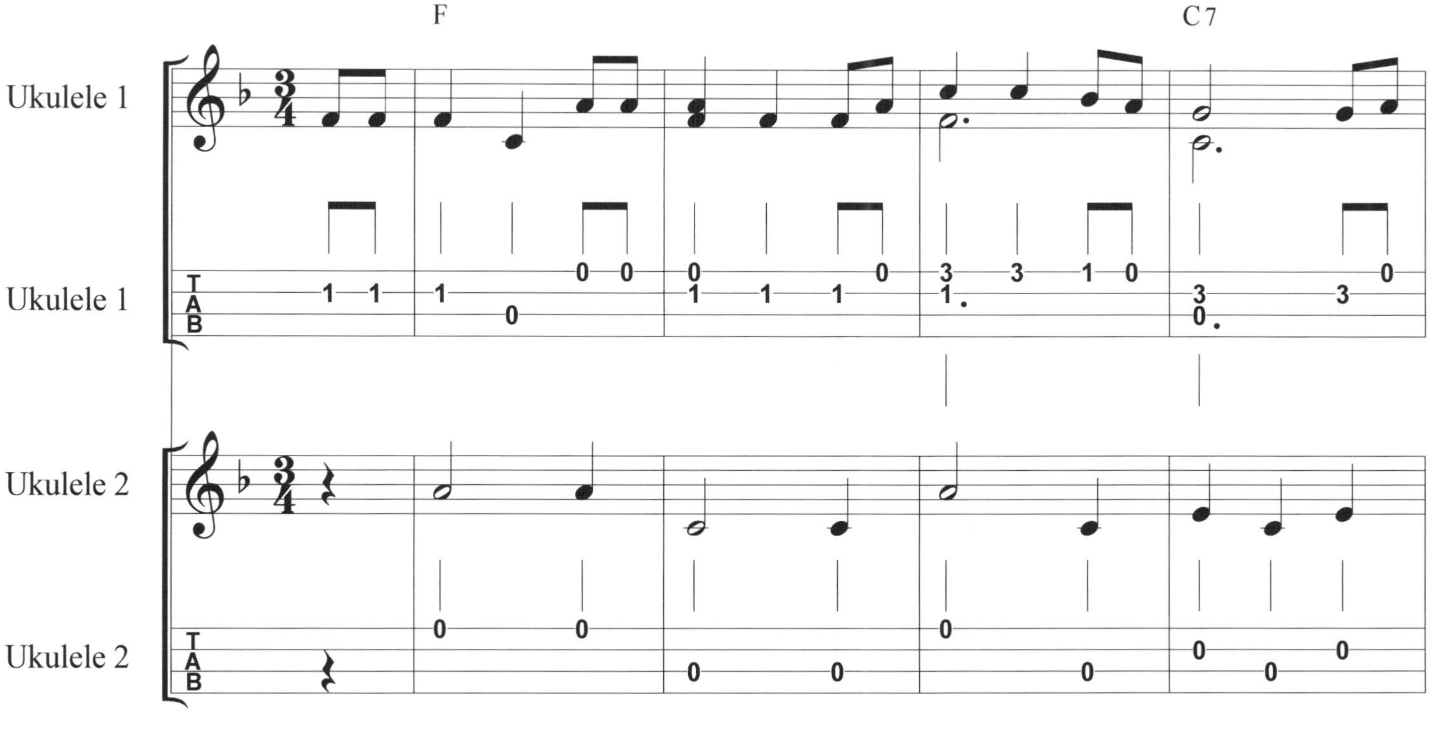

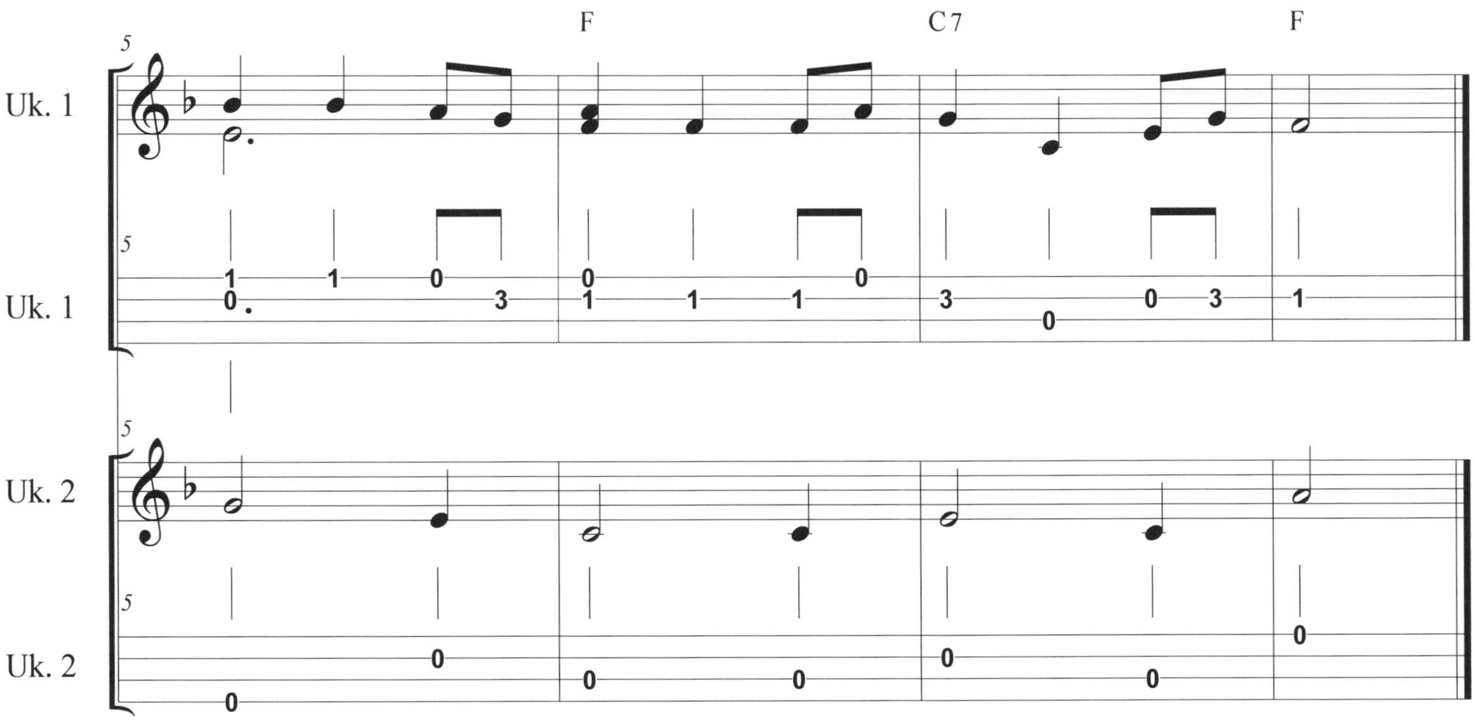

Oh, Sinner Man

Gospel

arr: Ondřej Šárek

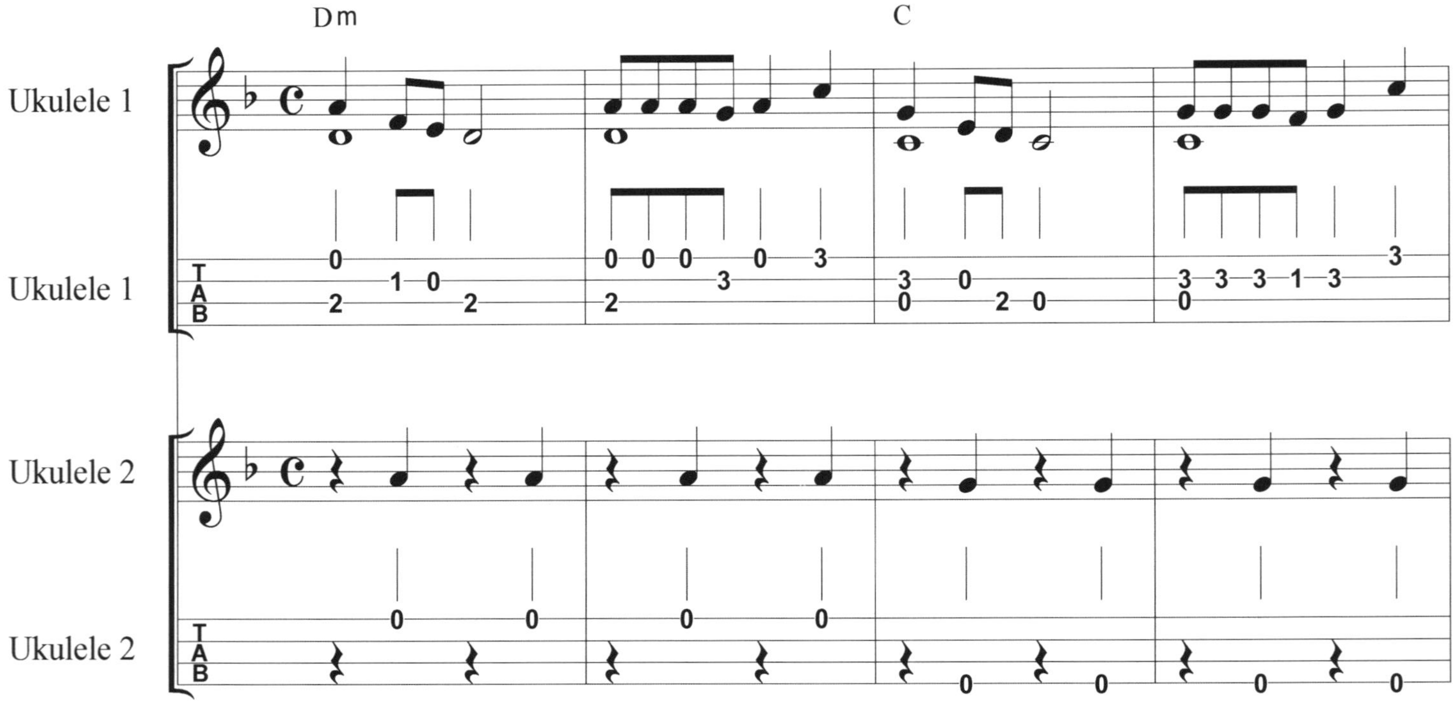

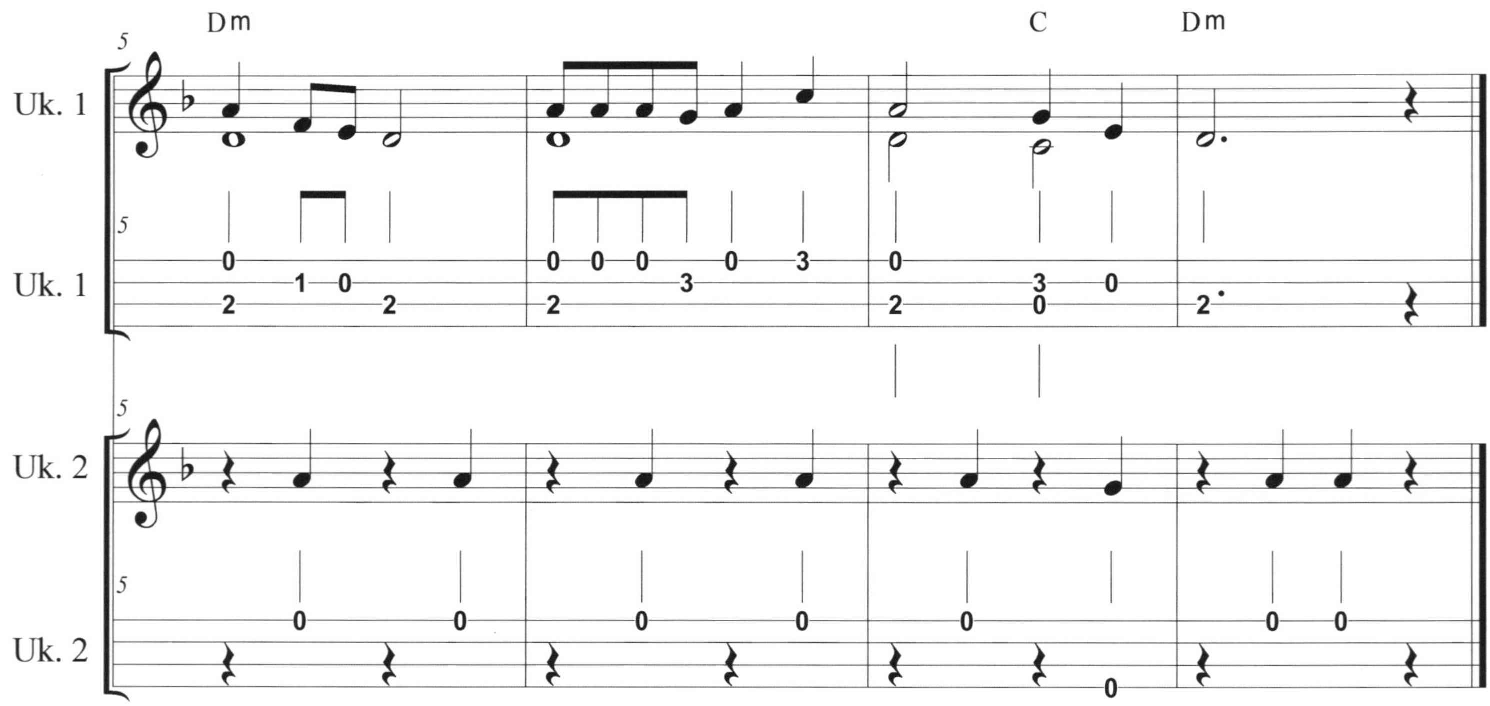

Reuben's Train

American folk song

arr: Ondřej Šárek

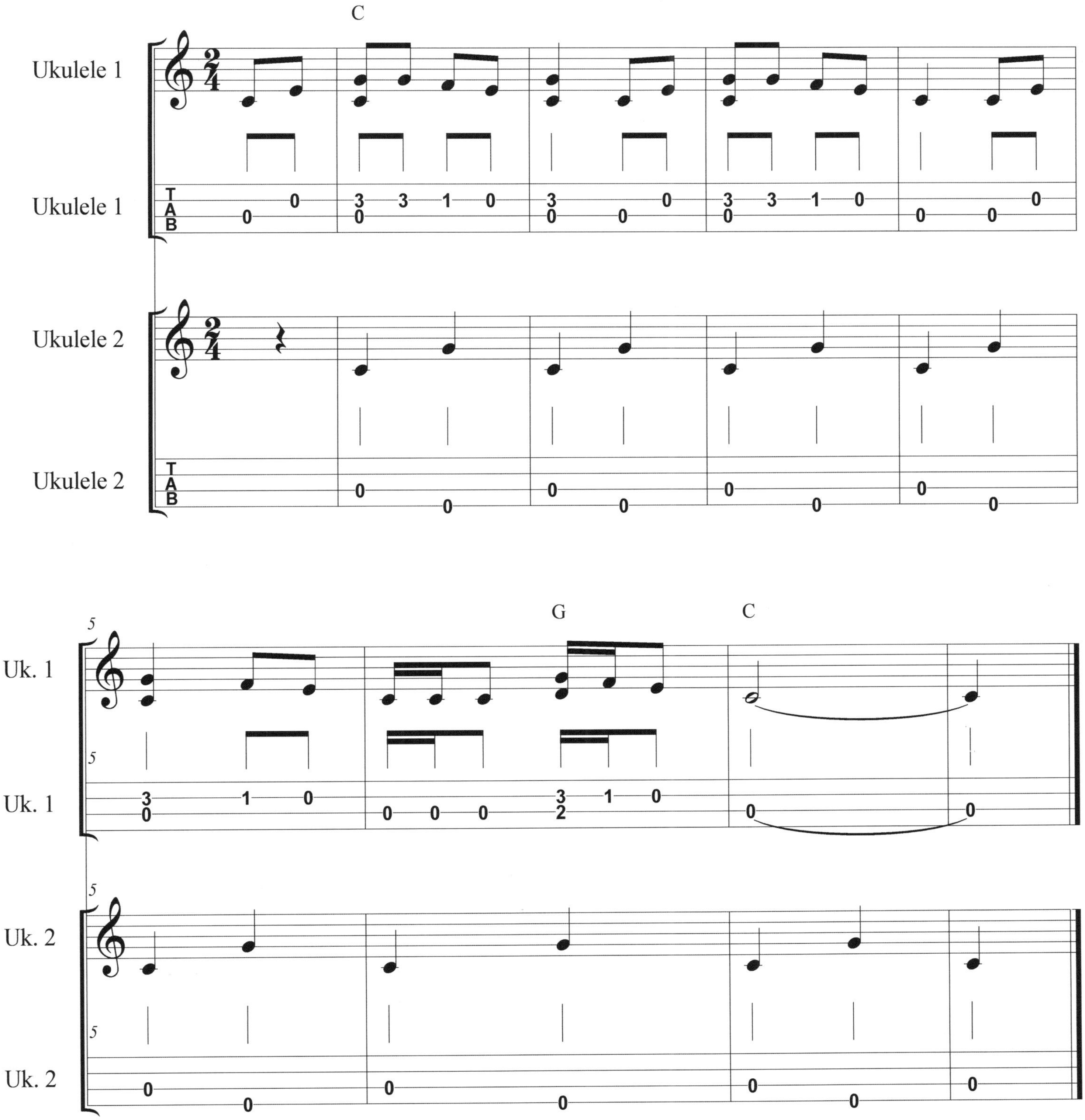

Te Deum

Marc-Antoine Charpentier (1643-1704)

arr: Ondřej Šárek

The Cruel War

American folk song
arr: Ondřej Šárek

Tom Dooley

American folk song
arr: Ondřej Šárek

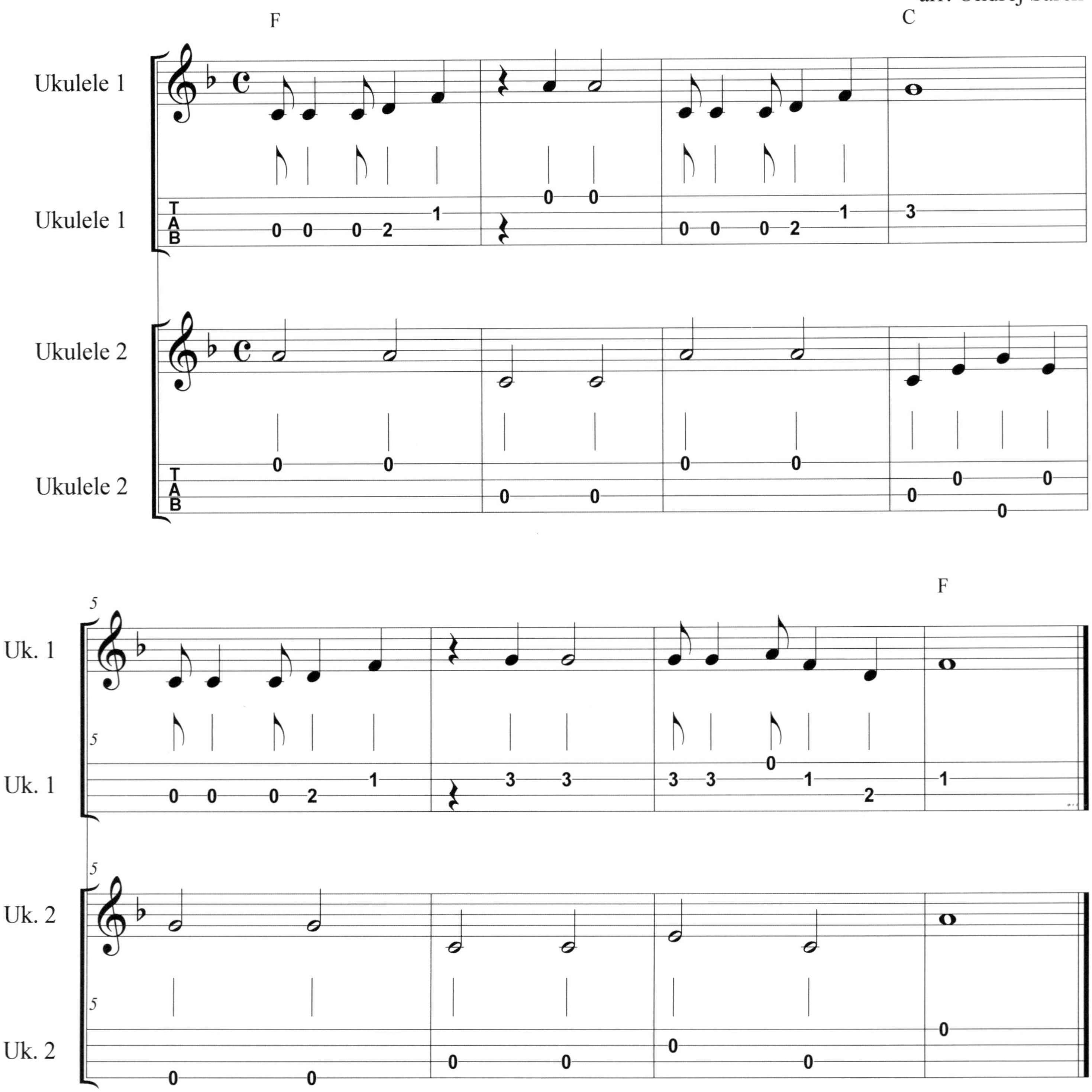

Who's Gonna Shoe Your Pretty Little Foot?

American folk song

arr: Ondřej Šárek

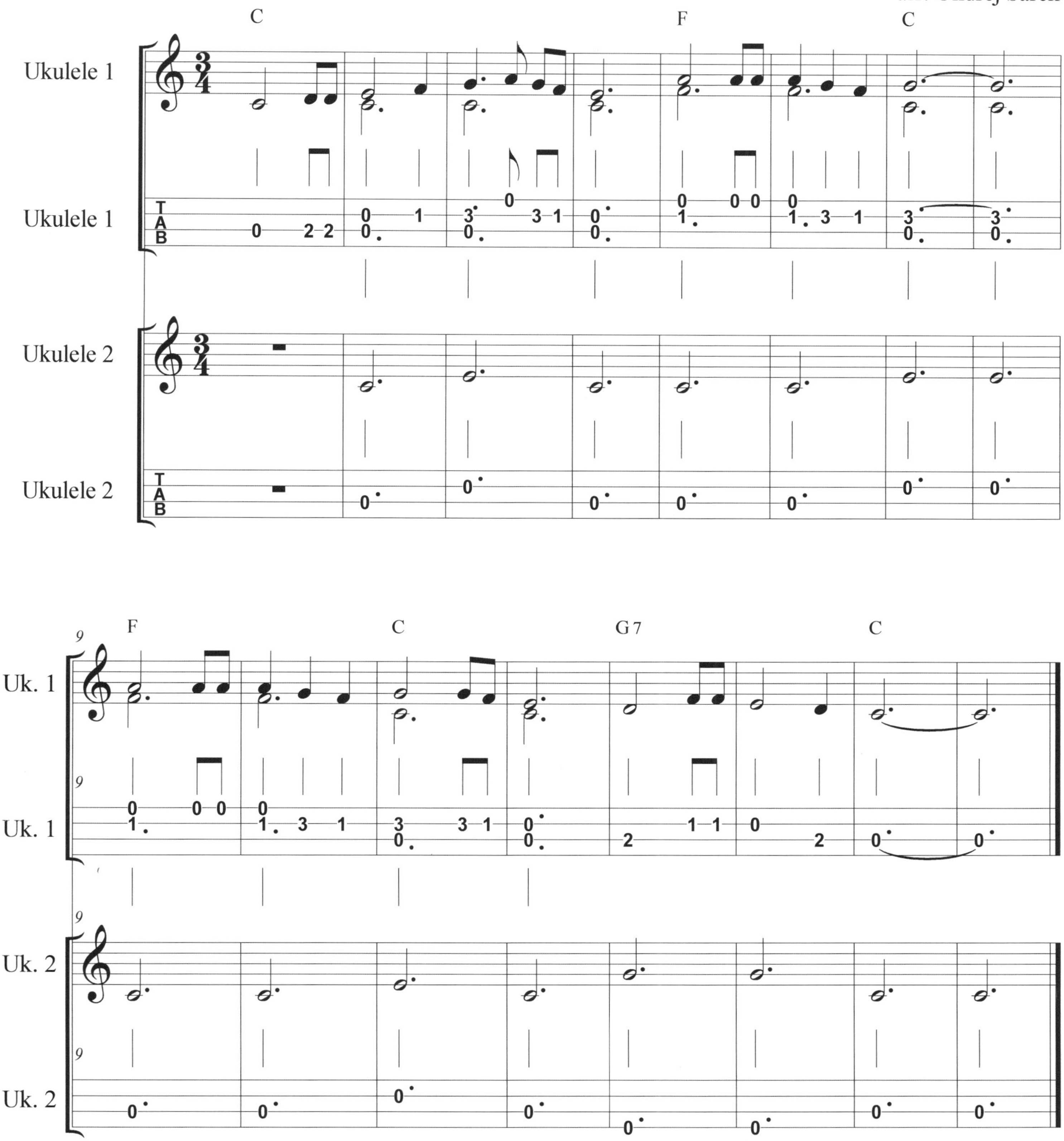

Aloha ‘Oe

Queen Liliuokalani (1838-1917)

arr: Ondřej Šárek

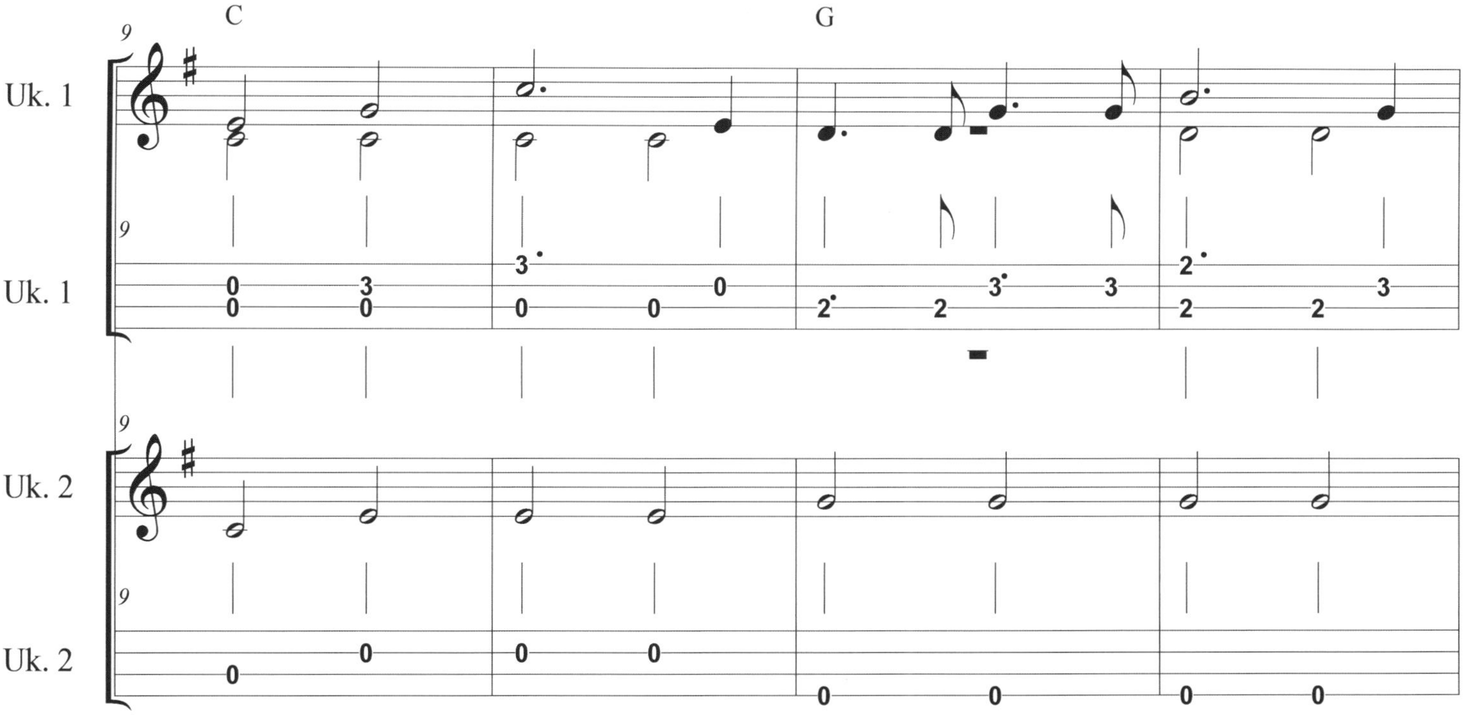
C
G
Uk. 1
Uk. 1
Uk. 2
Uk. 2

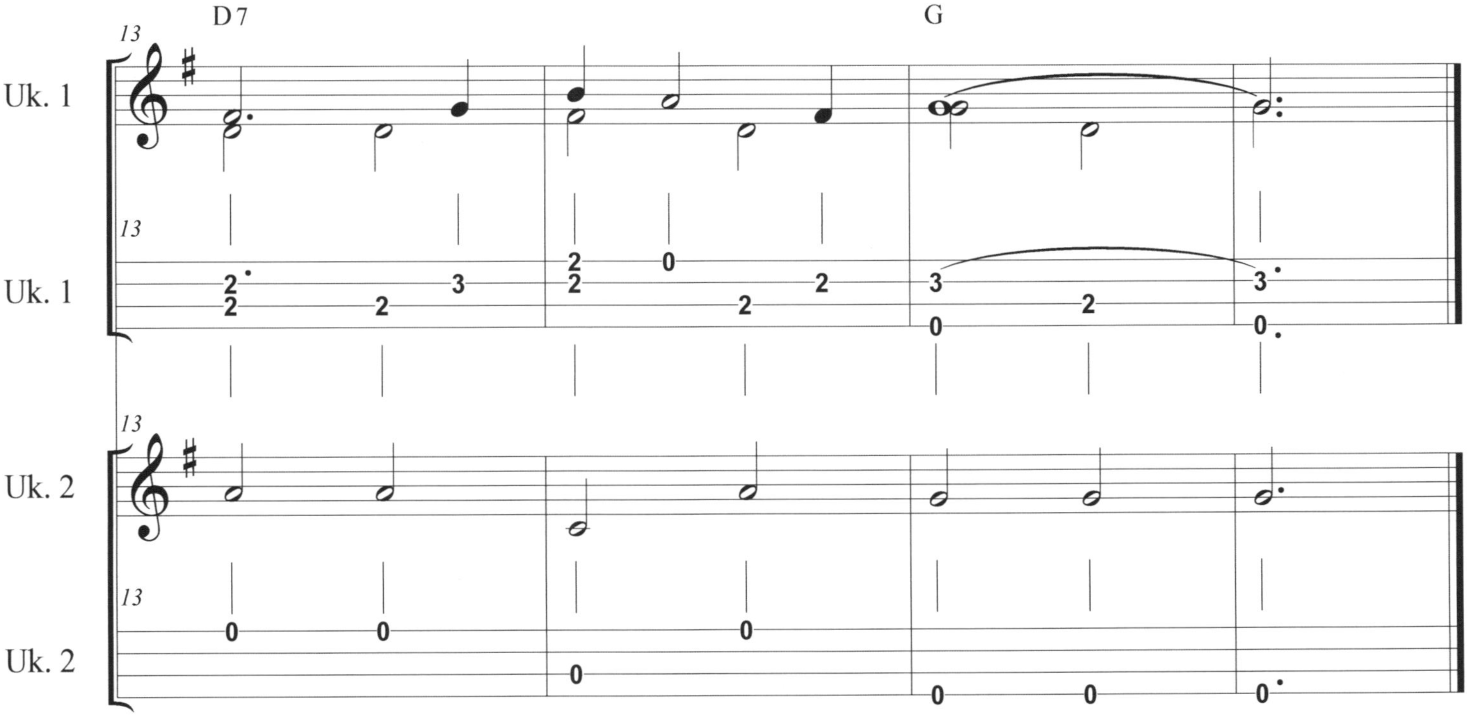
D 7
G
Uk. 1
Uk. 1
Uk. 2
Uk. 2

Au clair de la Lune

French folk song
arr: Ondřej Šárek

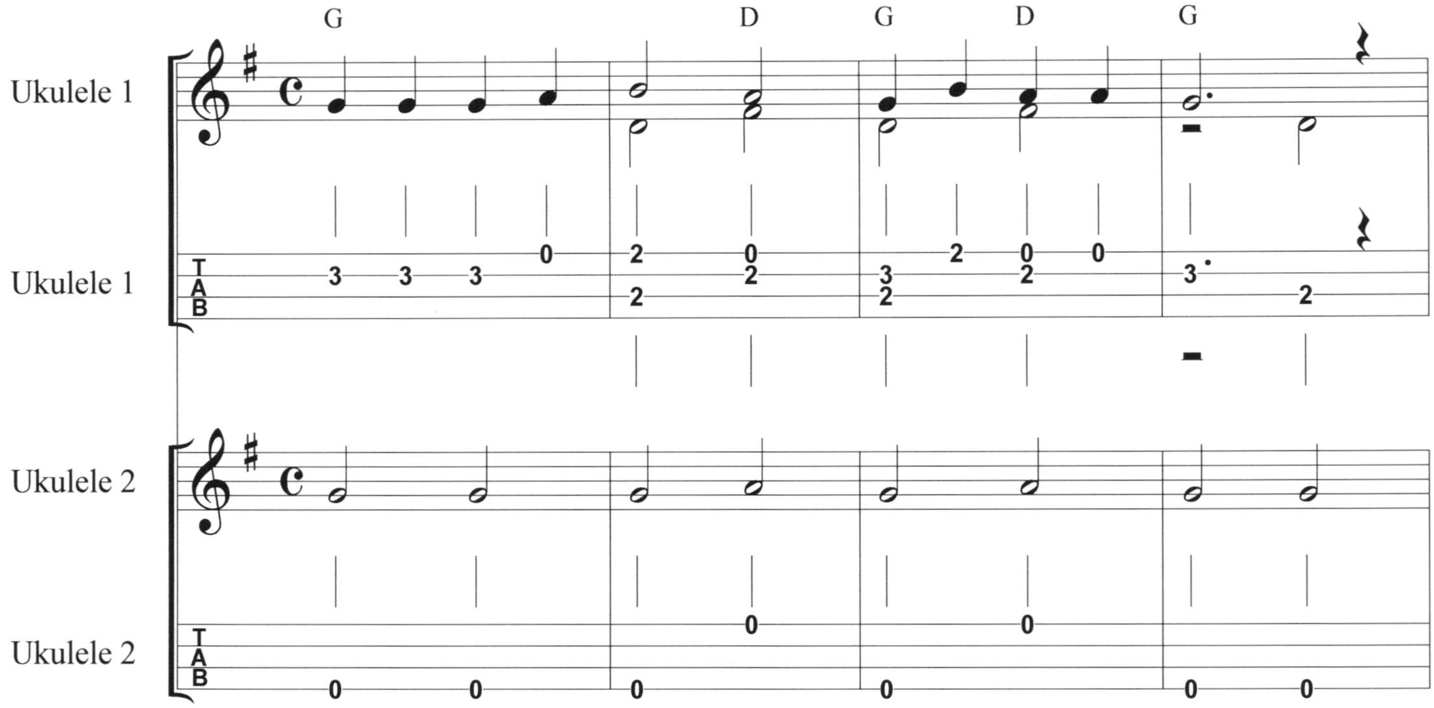

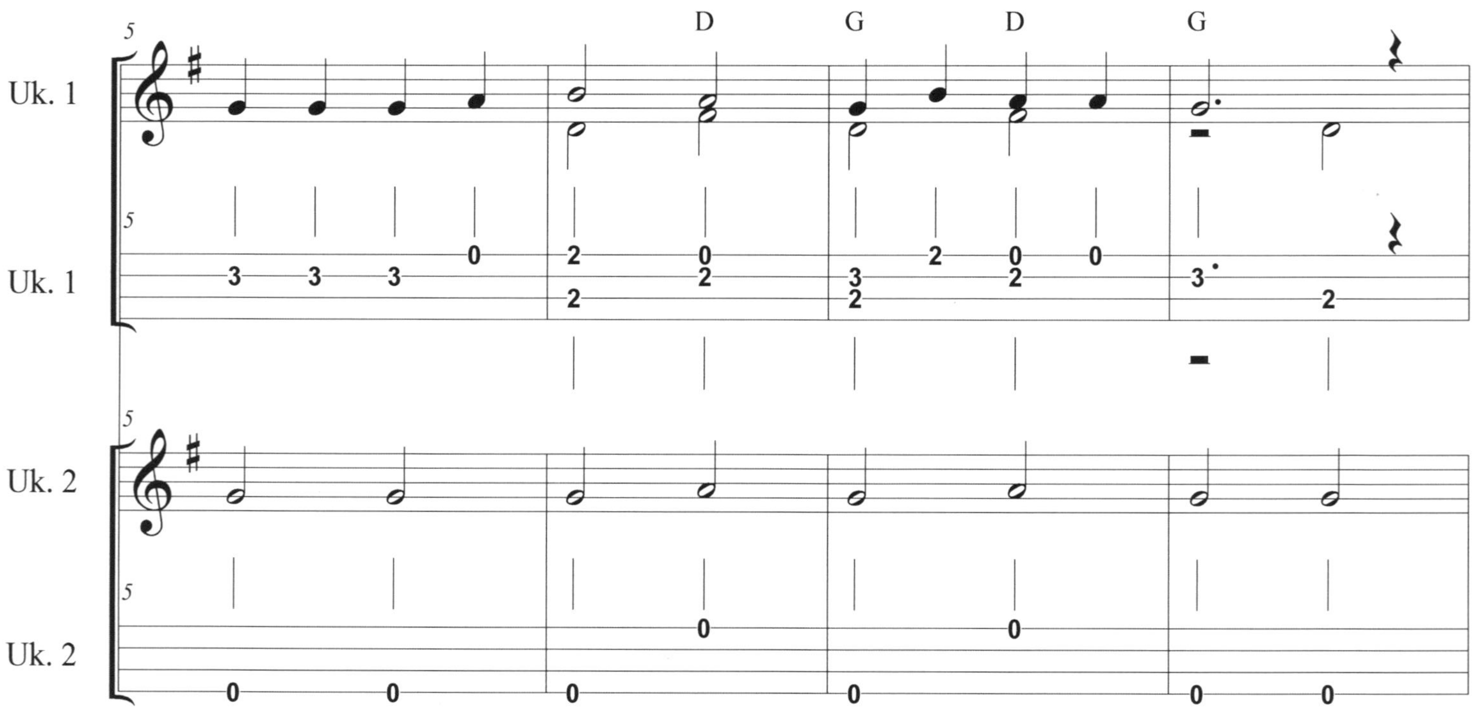

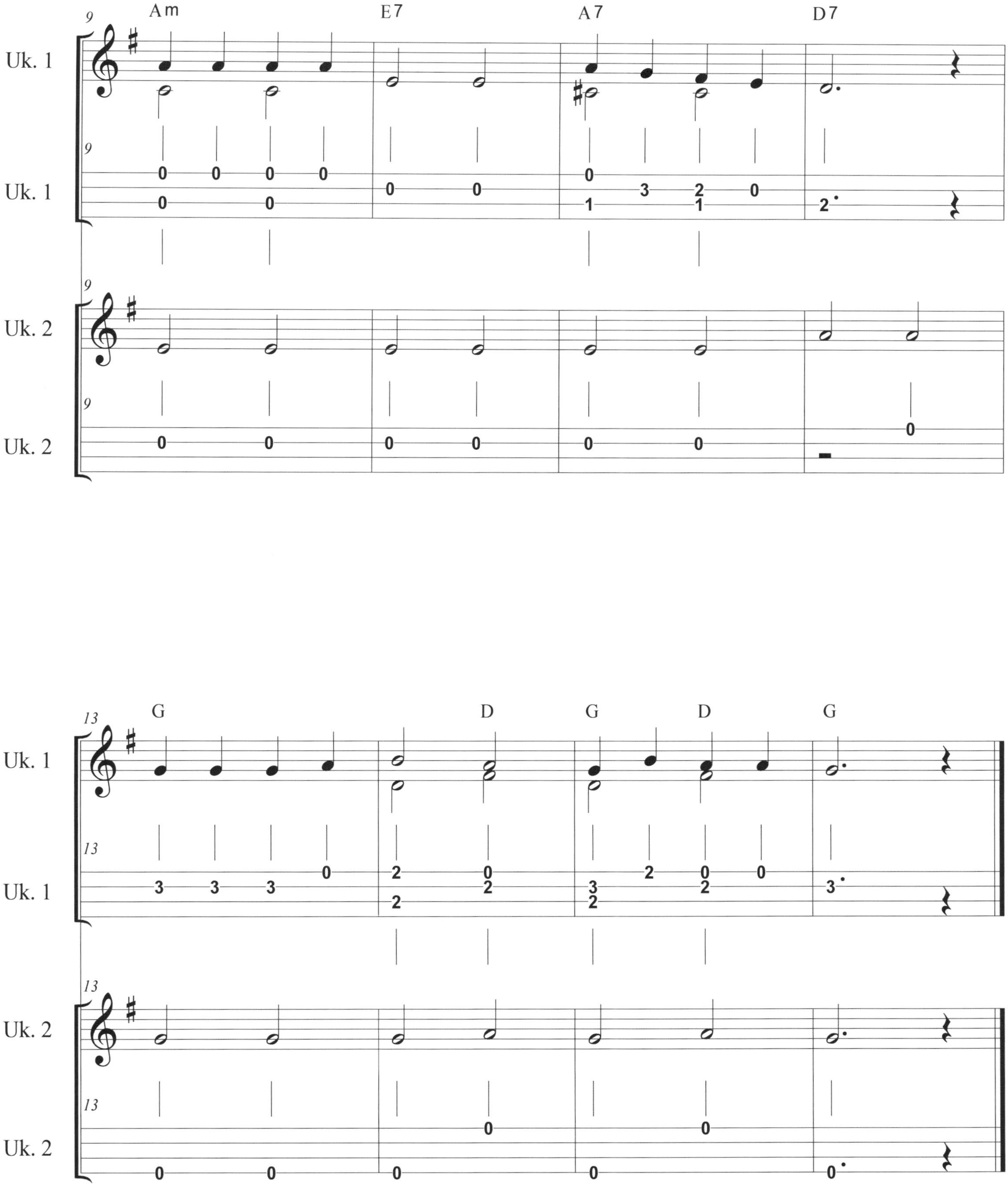
Uk. 1
Uk. 2
Am
E7
A7
D7
G
D
G
D
G

Aura Lee

American folk song
arr: Ondřej Šárek

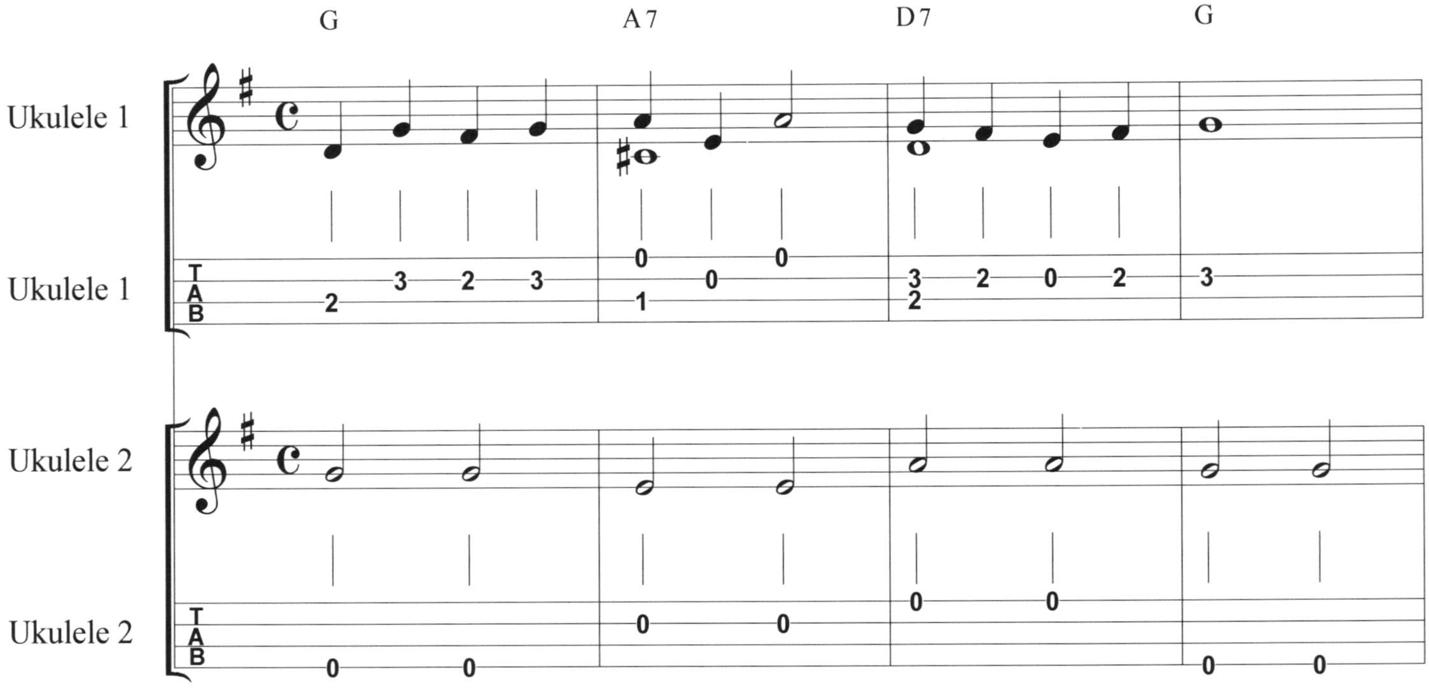

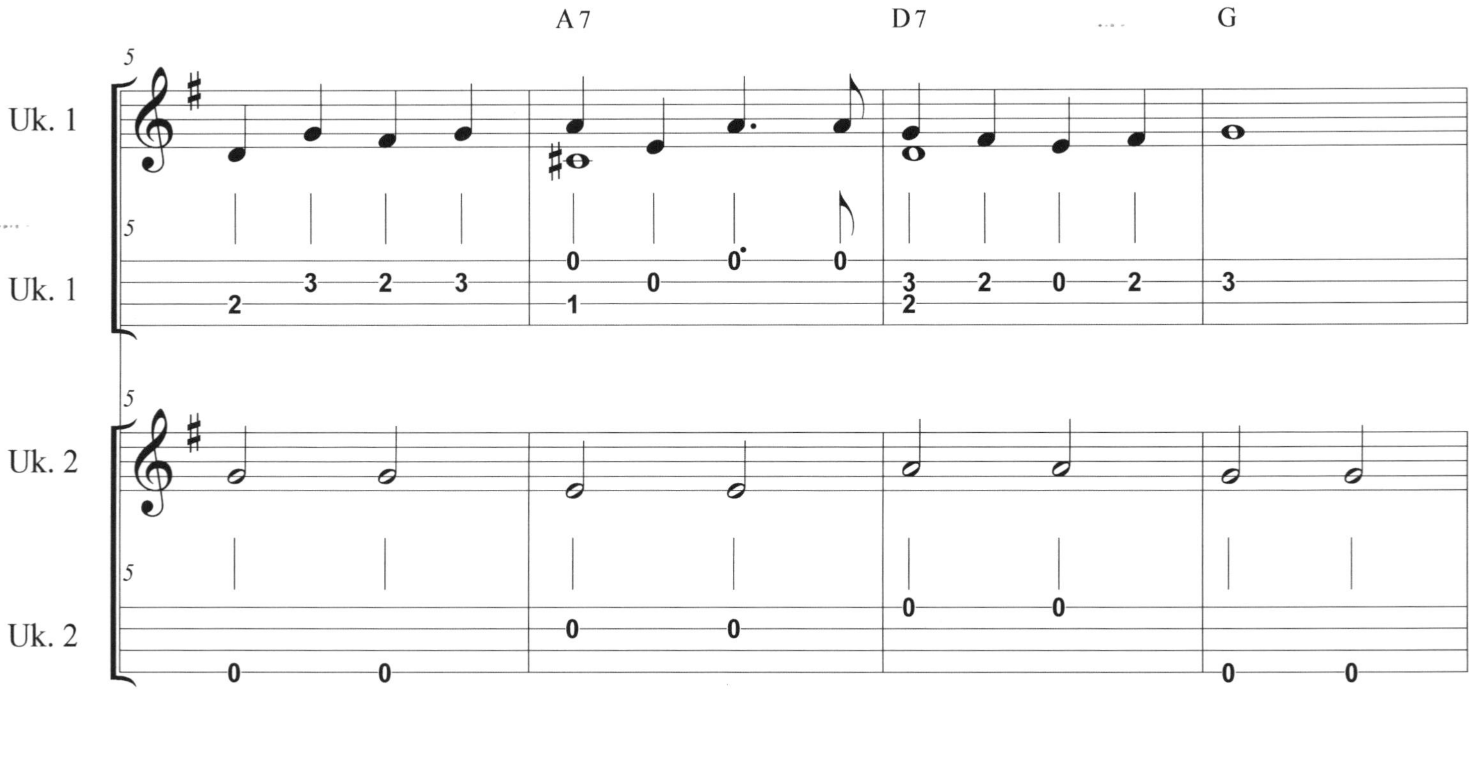

Uk. 1
Uk. 2
B7
Em
B7
G
E7
A7
D7
G

Camptown Races

Stephen Foster (1826-1864)
arr: Ondřej Šárek

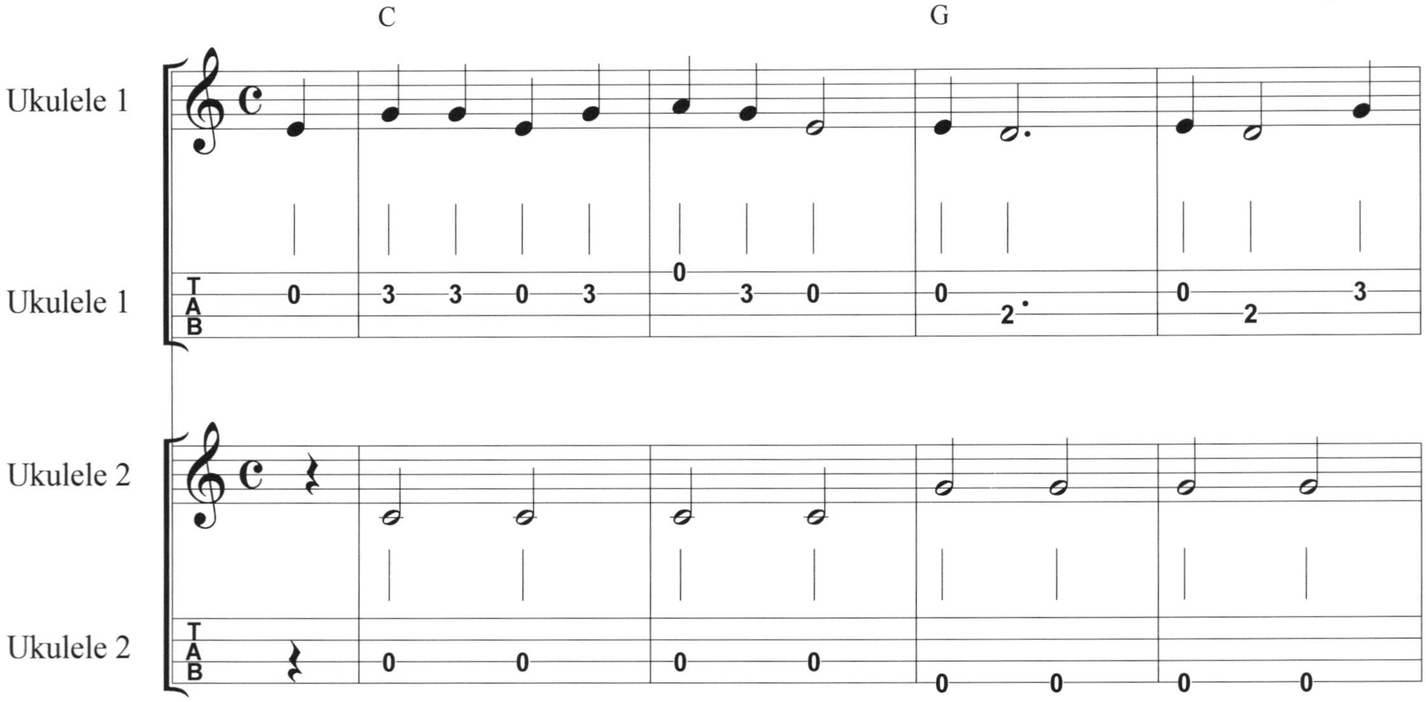

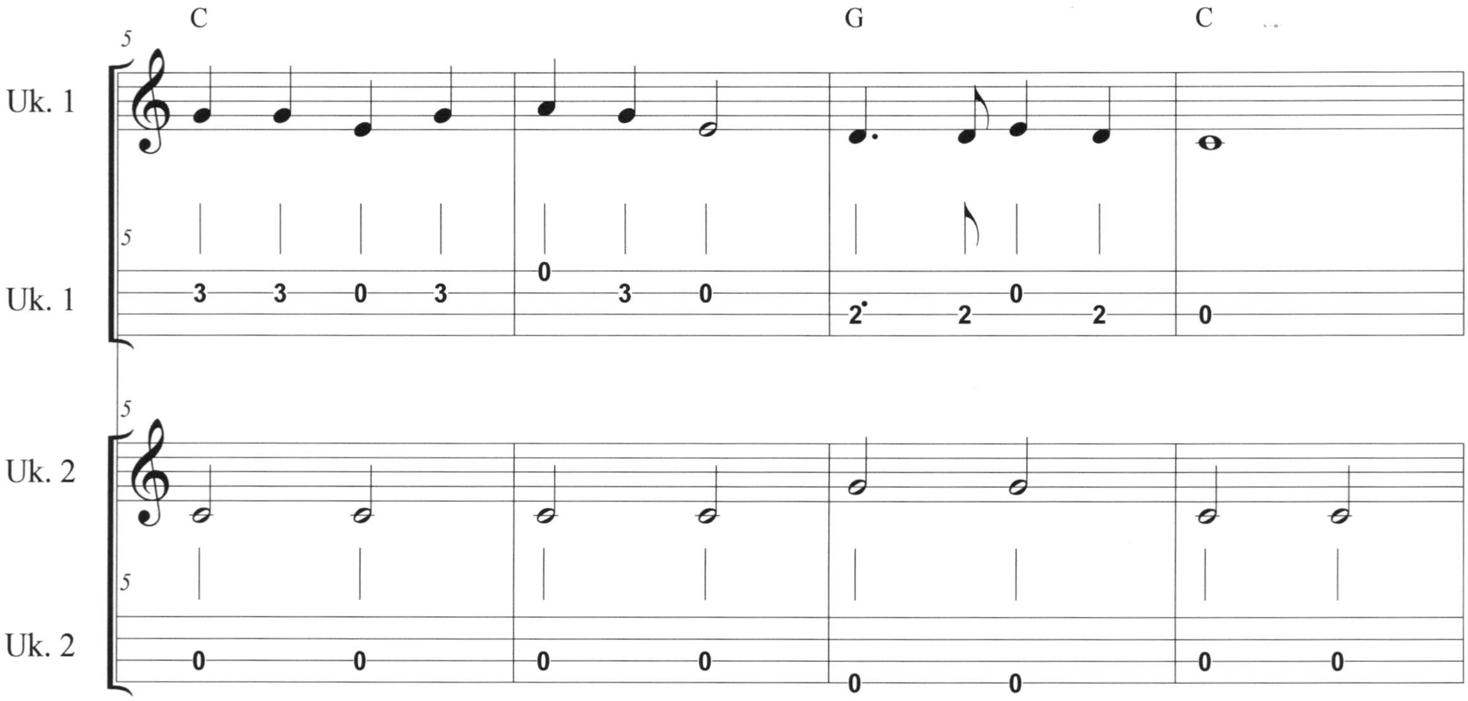

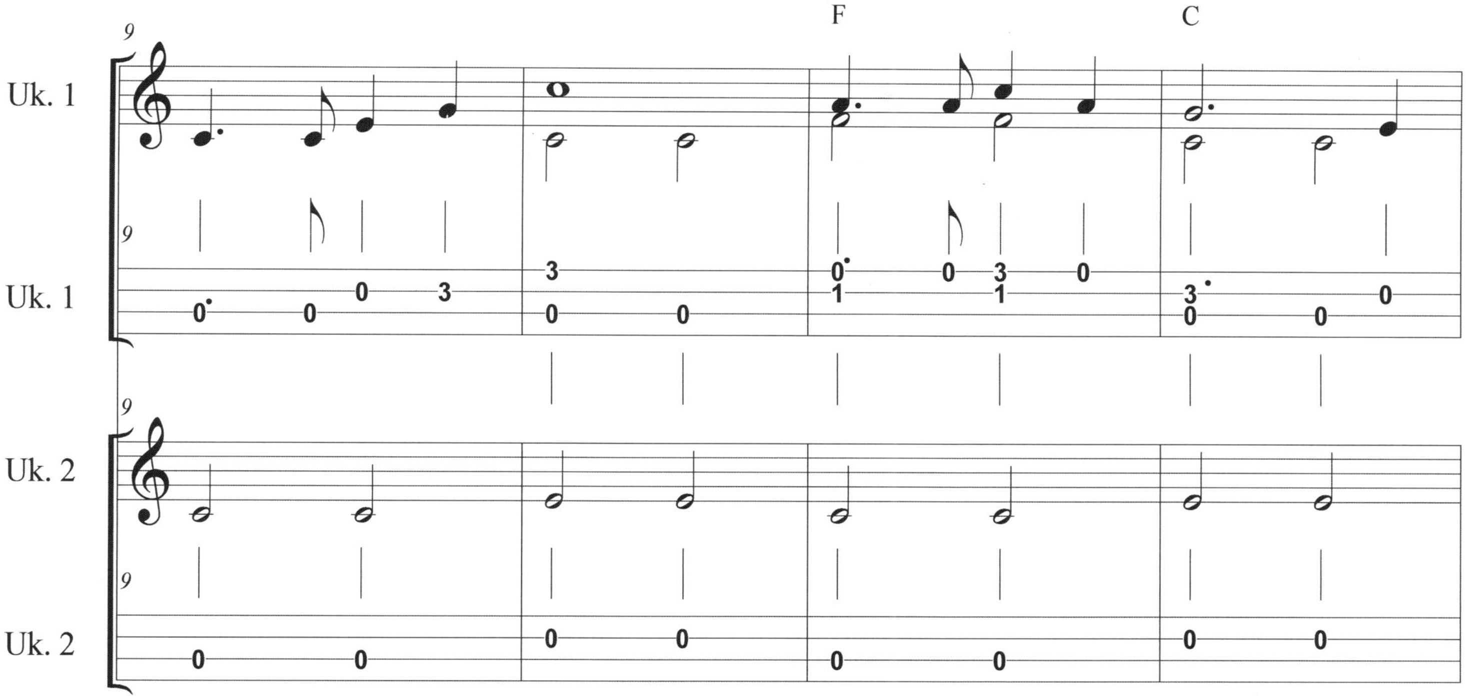
9
F
C
Uk. 1
Uk. 1
Uk. 2
Uk. 2

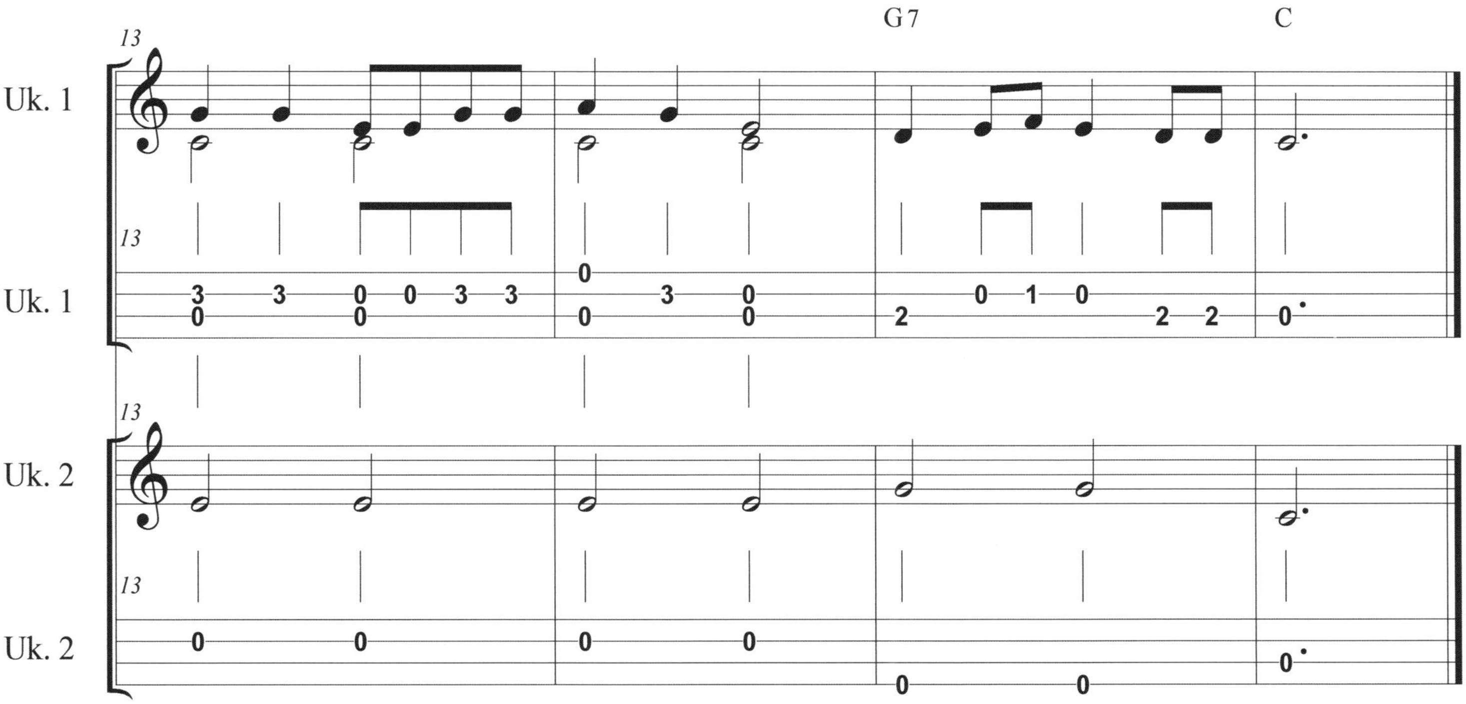
13
G 7
C
Uk. 1
Uk. 1
Uk. 2
Uk. 2

Ding! Dong!

English carol
arr: Ondřej Šárek

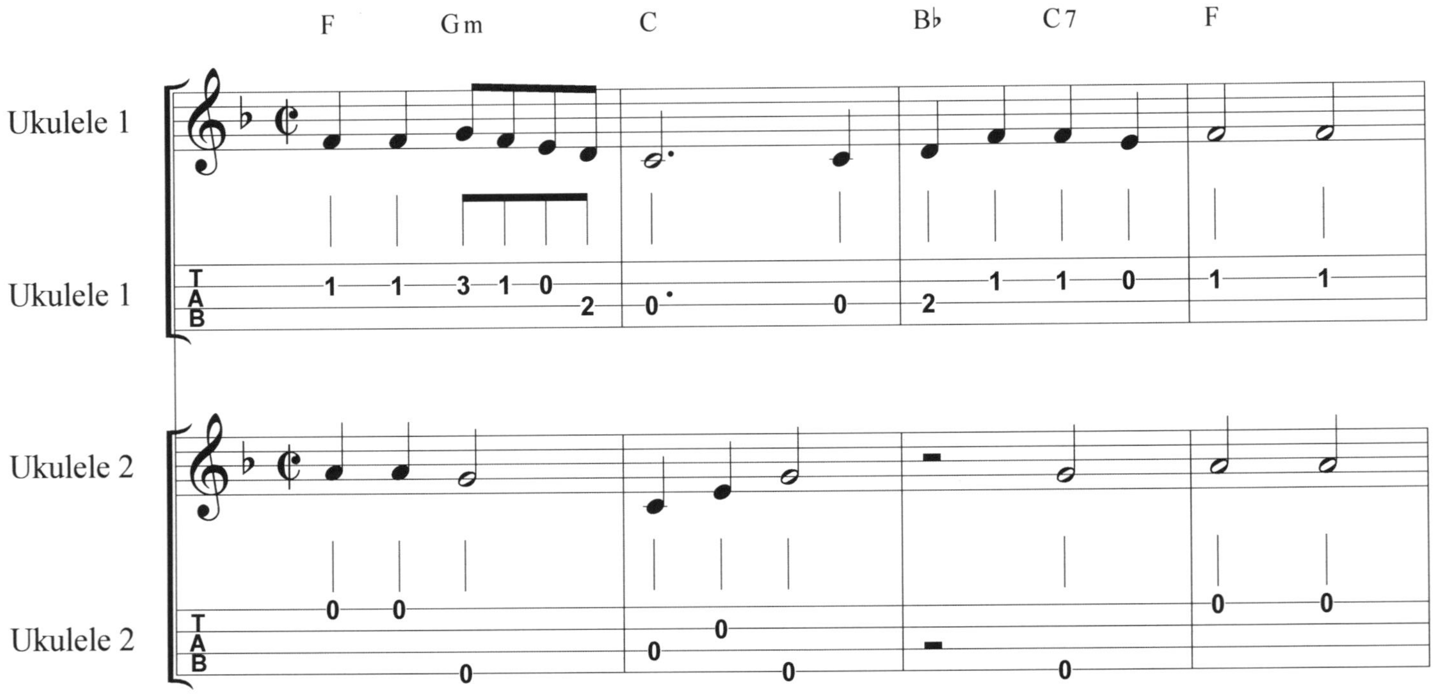

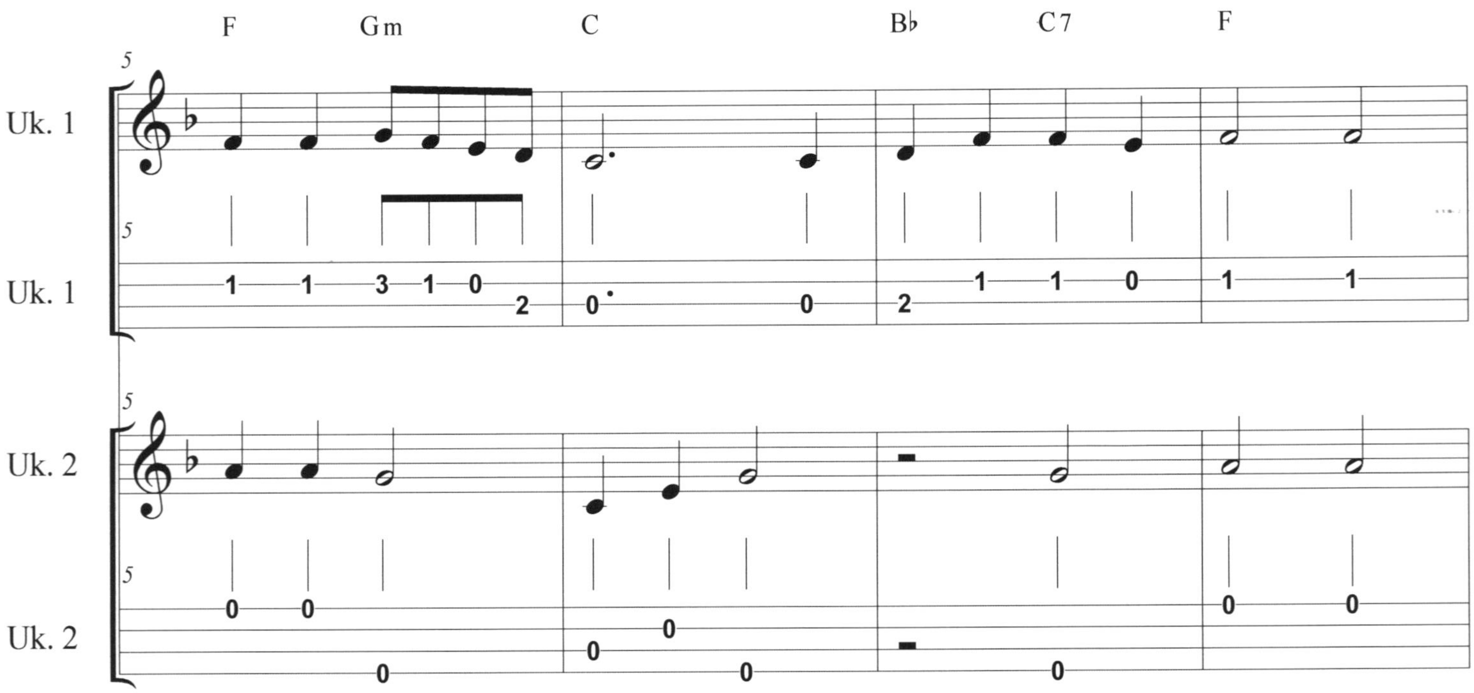

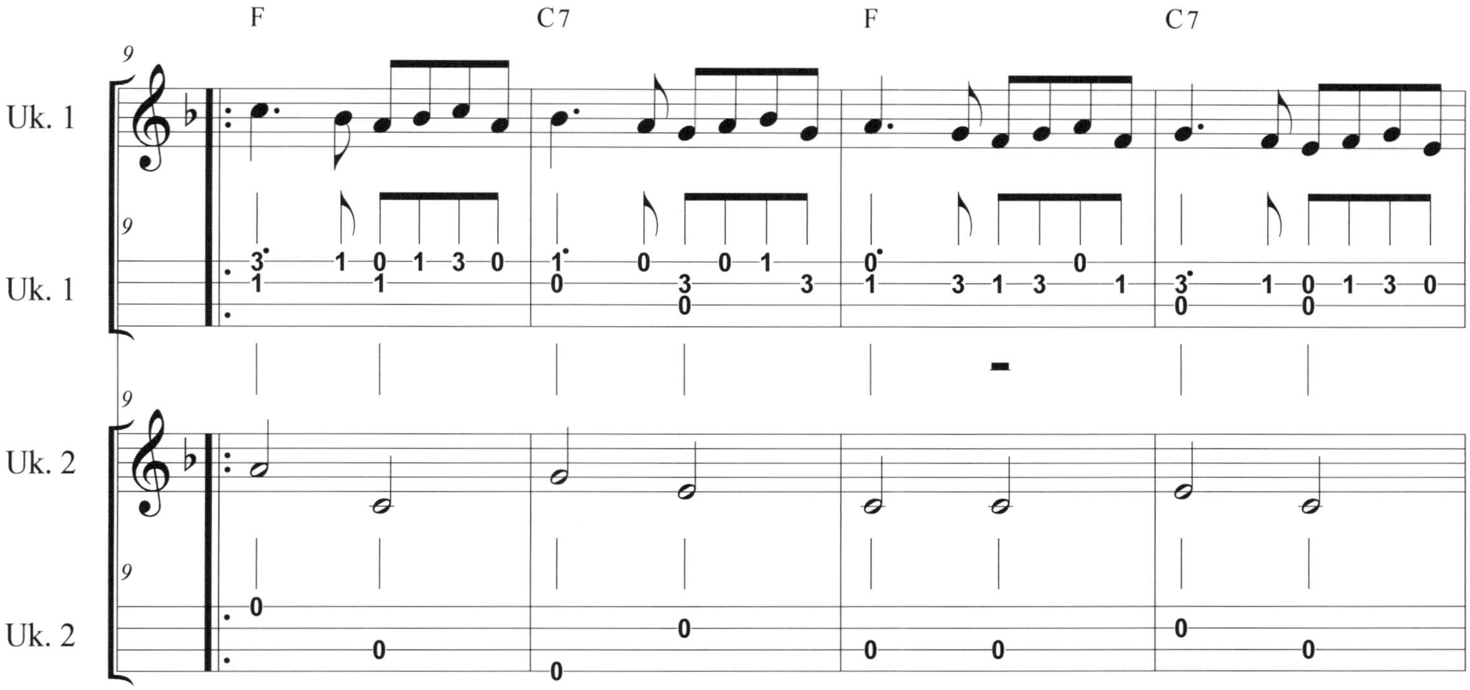
F
C7
F
C7
Uk. 1
Uk. 1
Uk. 2
Uk. 2

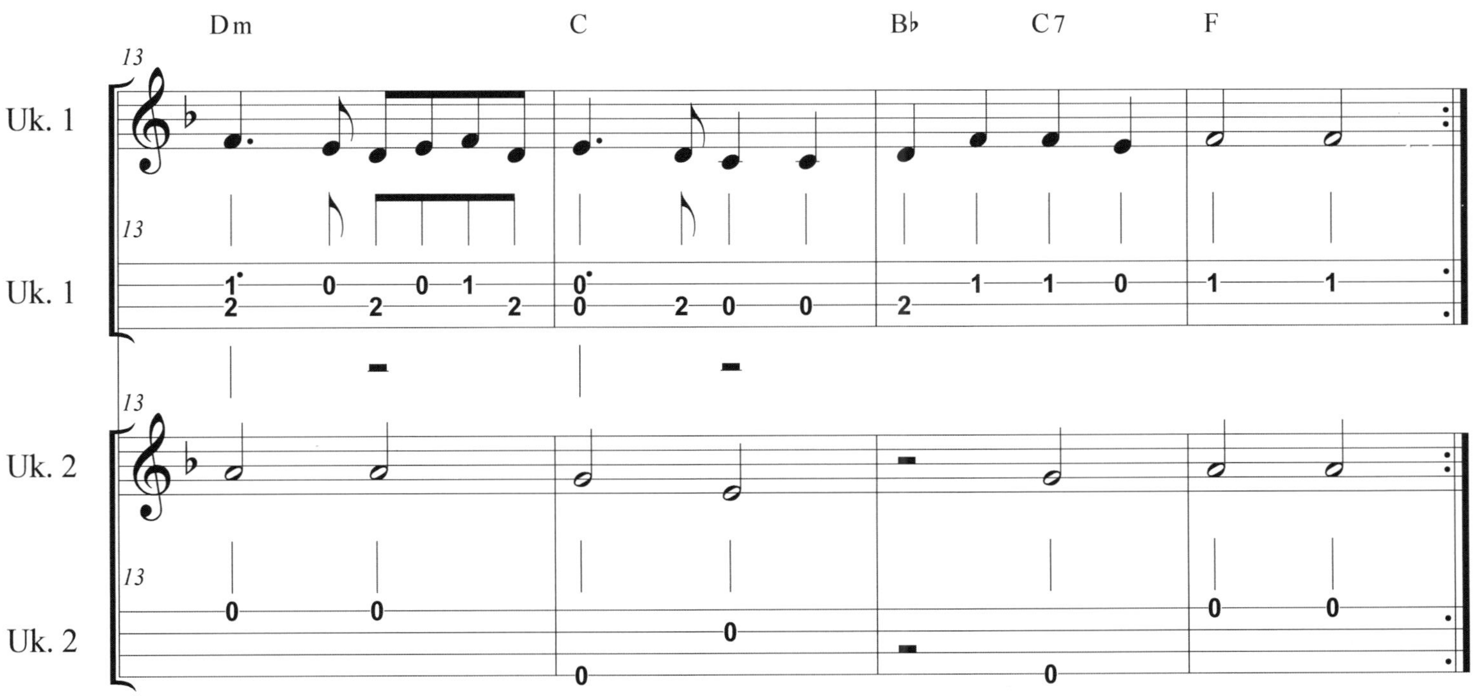
Dm
C
B♭
C7
F
Uk. 1
Uk. 1
Uk. 2
Uk. 2

Good King Wenceslas

English carol

arr: Ondřej Šárek

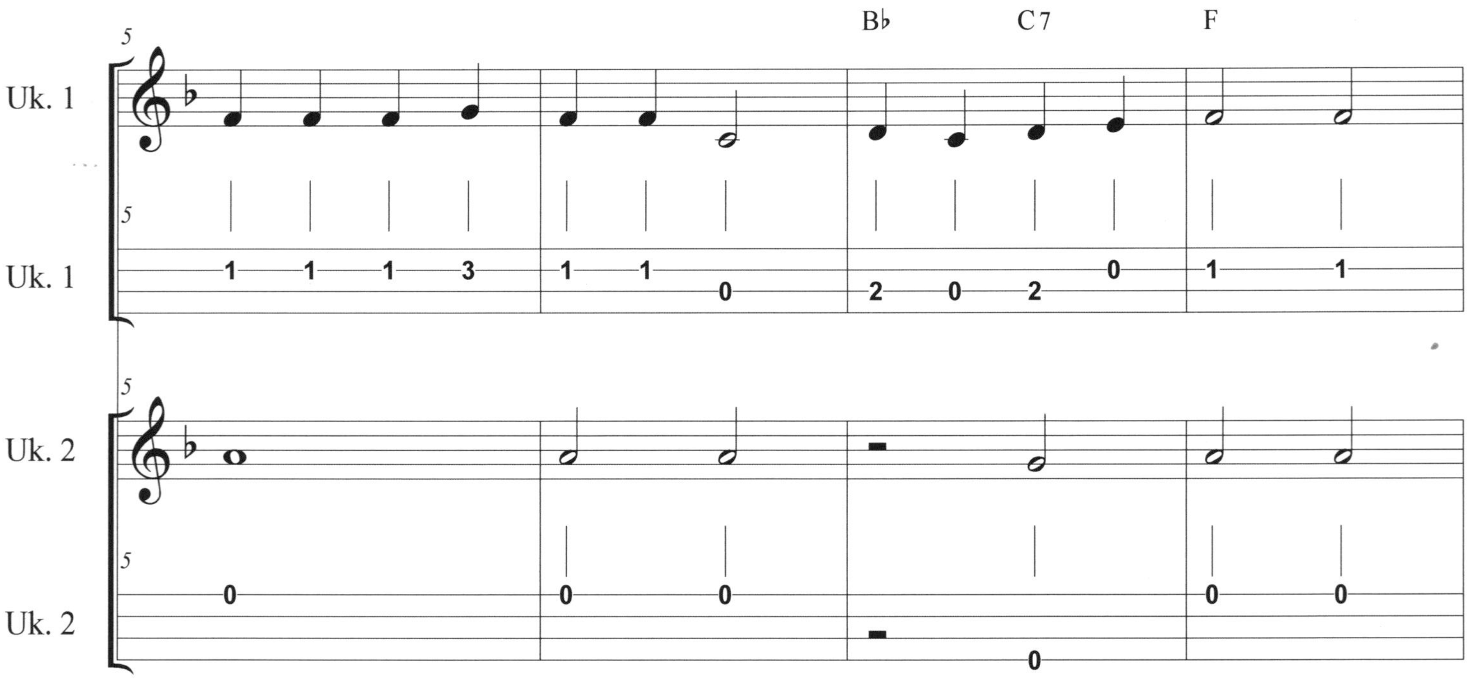

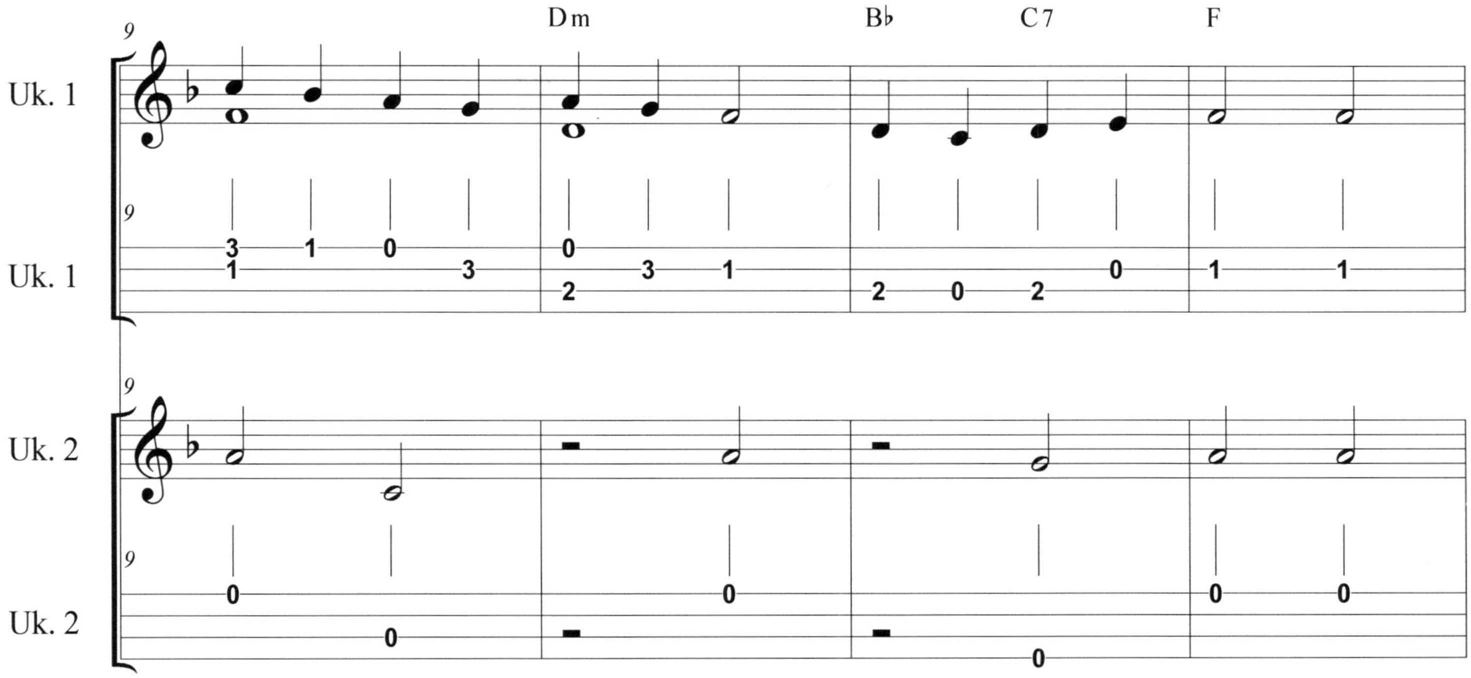
9
Dm
B♭
C7
F
Uk. 1
Uk. 1
Uk. 2
Uk. 2

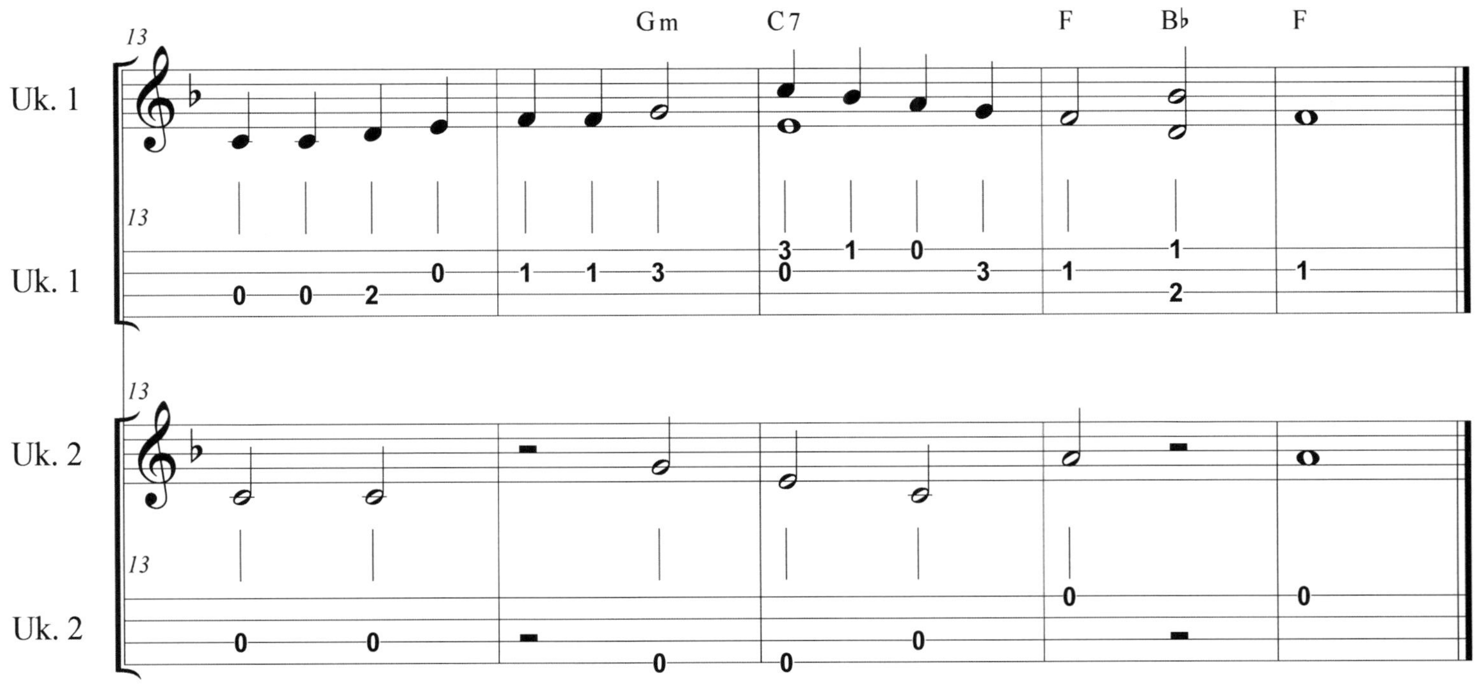
13
Gm
C7
F
B♭
F
Uk. 1
Uk. 1
Uk. 2
Uk. 2

Lullaby

Johannes Brahms (1833-1897)
arr: Ondřej Šárek

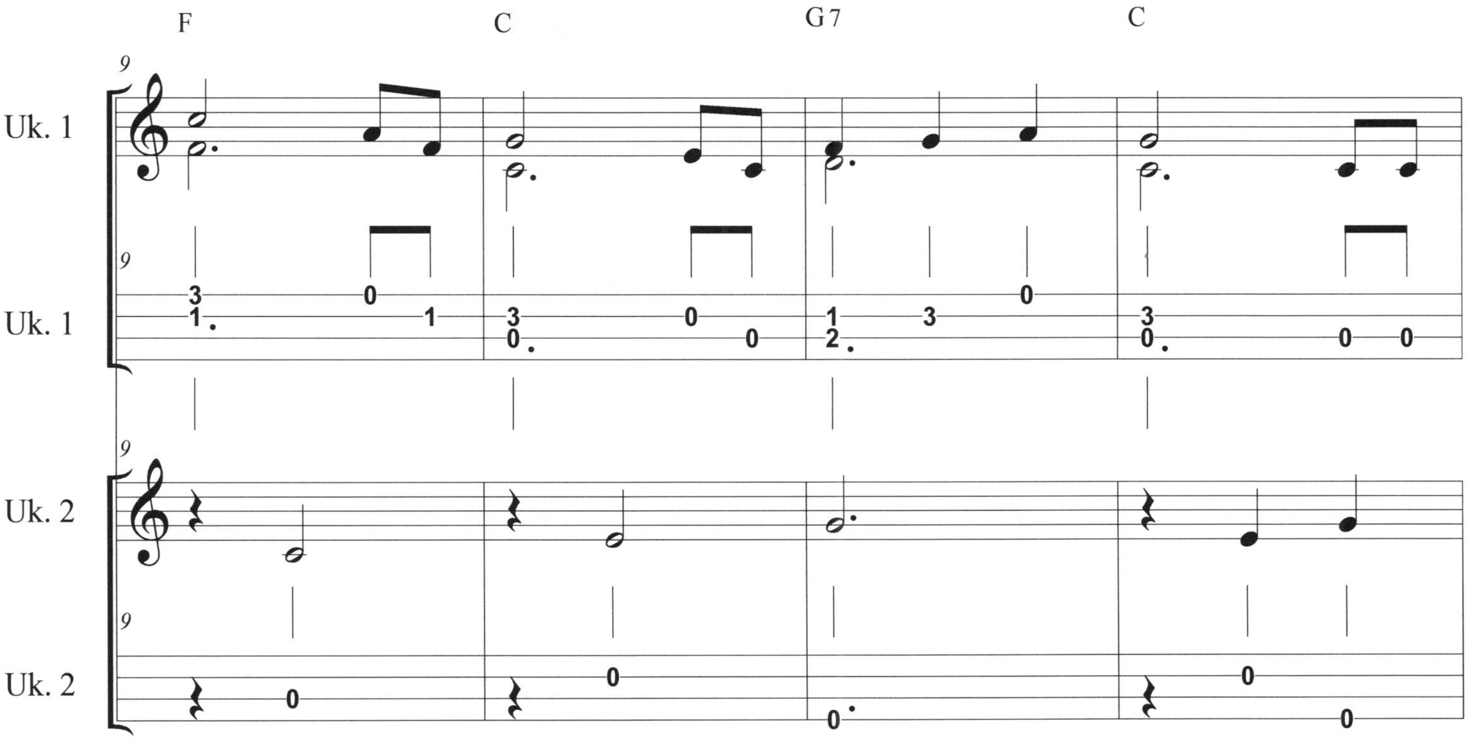
F
C
G7
C
Uk. 1
Uk. 1
Uk. 2
Uk. 2

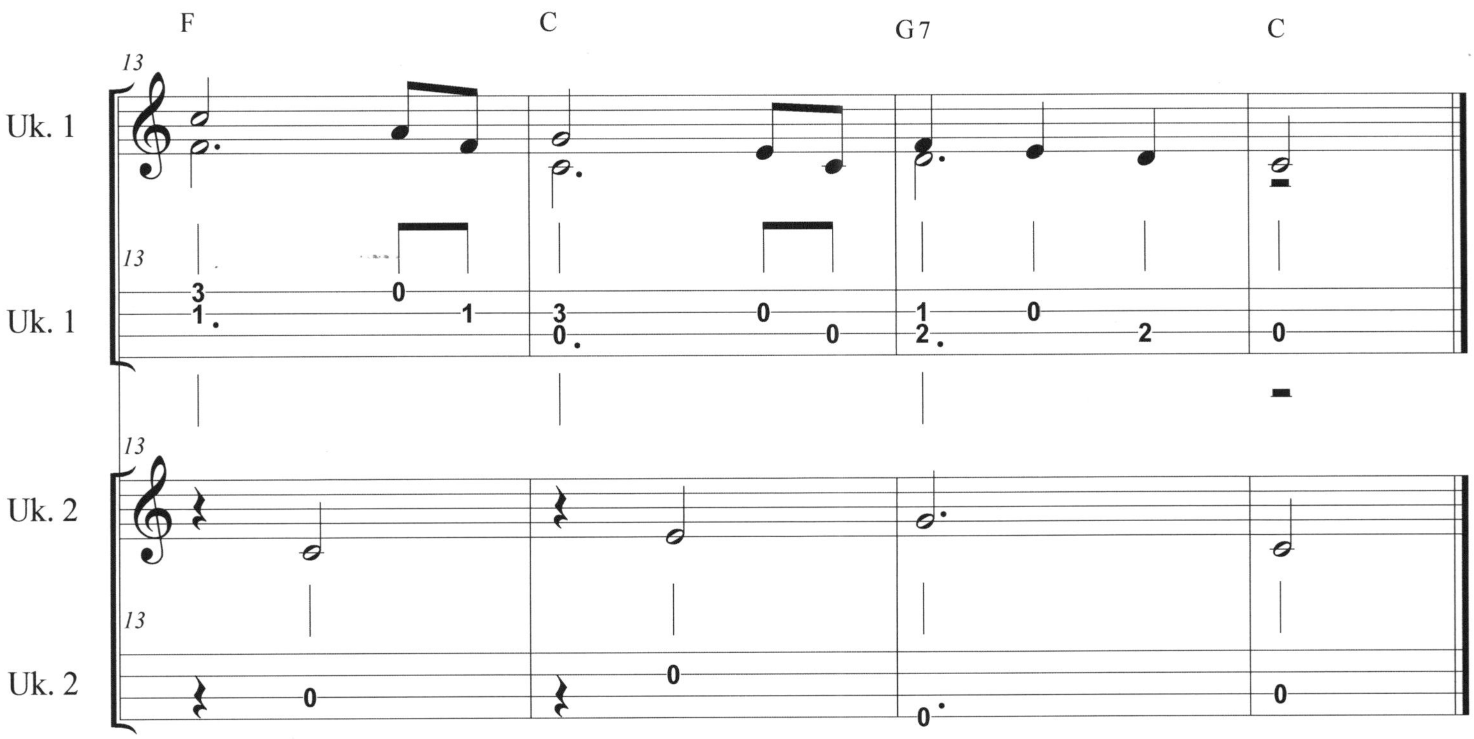
F
C
G7
C
Uk. 1
Uk. 1
Uk. 2
Uk. 2

MacPherson's Farewell

Scottish folk song
arr: Ondřej Šárek

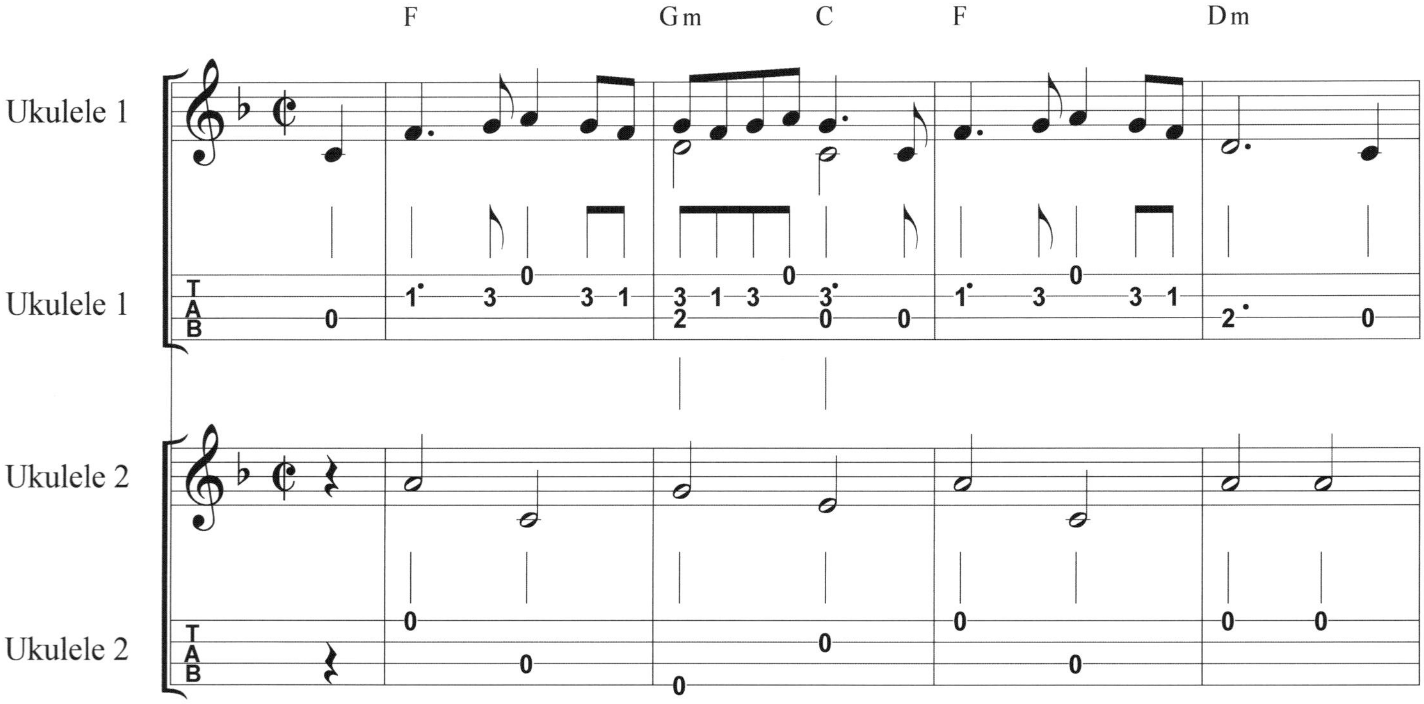

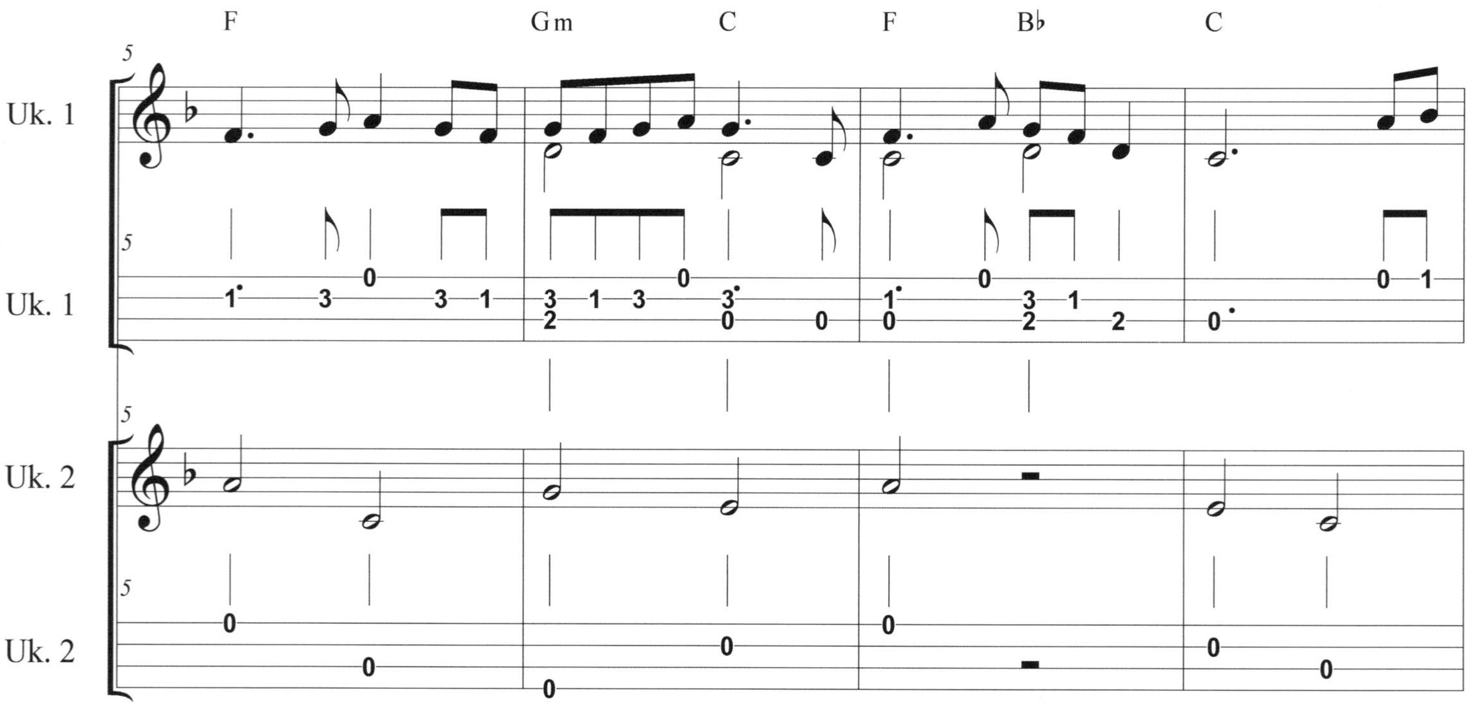

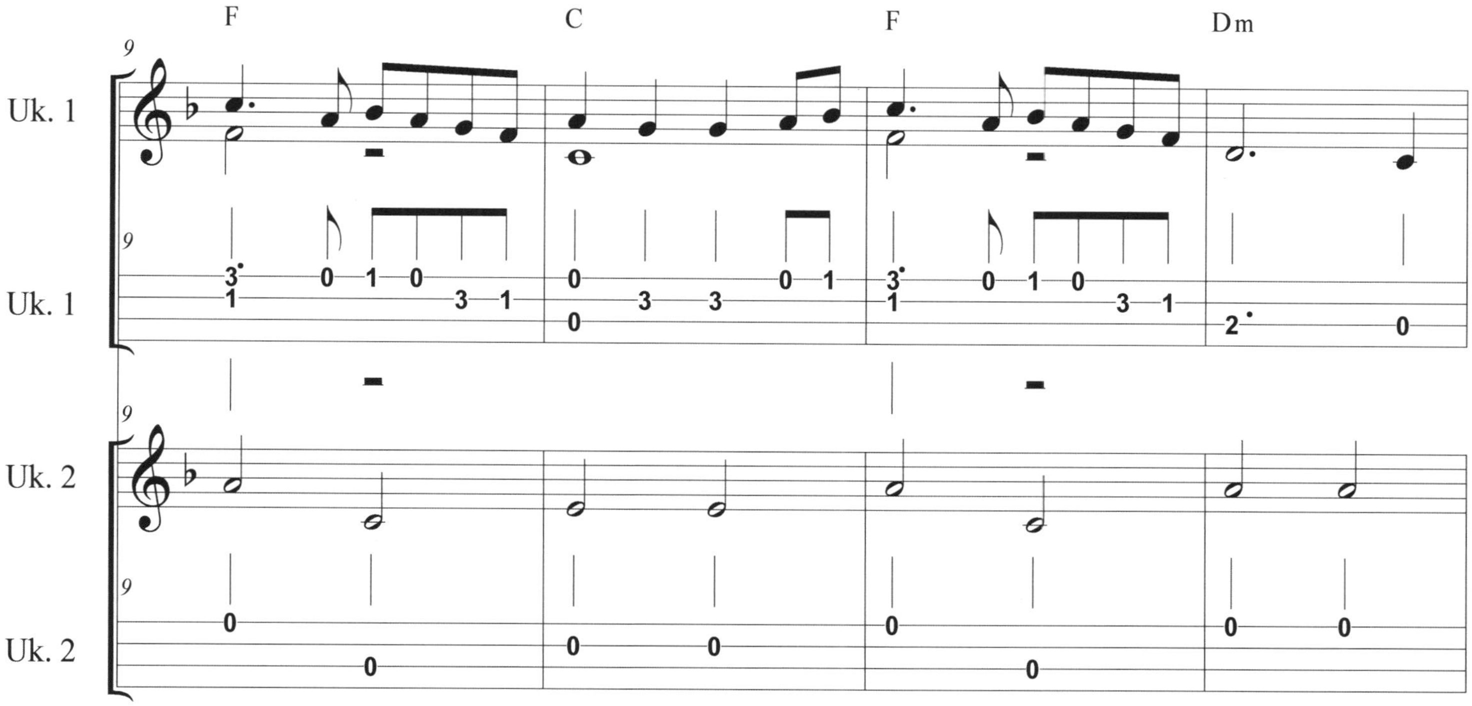
F
C
F
Dm
Uk. 1
Uk. 1
Uk. 2
Uk. 2

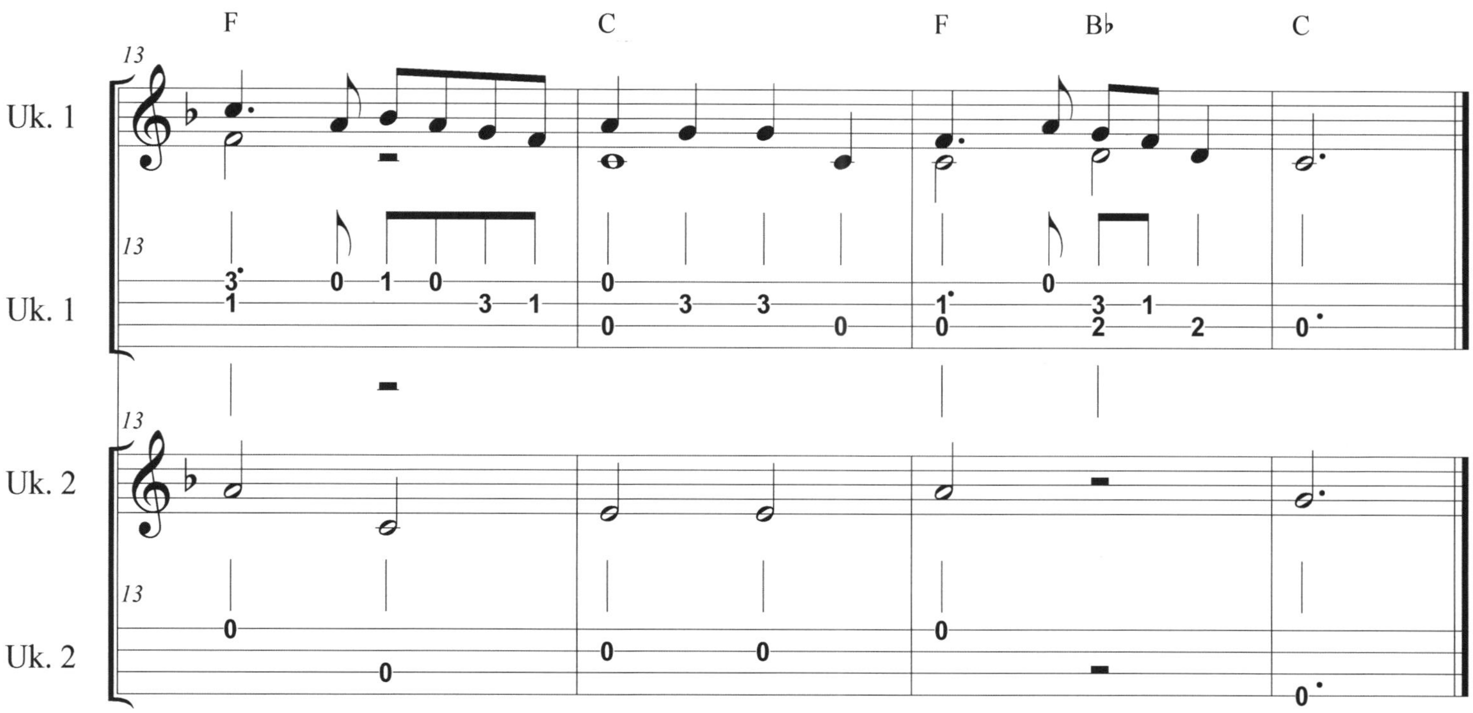
F
C
F
B♭
C
Uk. 1
Uk. 1
Uk. 2
Uk. 2

Ode to Joy

Ludwig van Beethoven (1770-1827)
arr: Ondřej Šárek

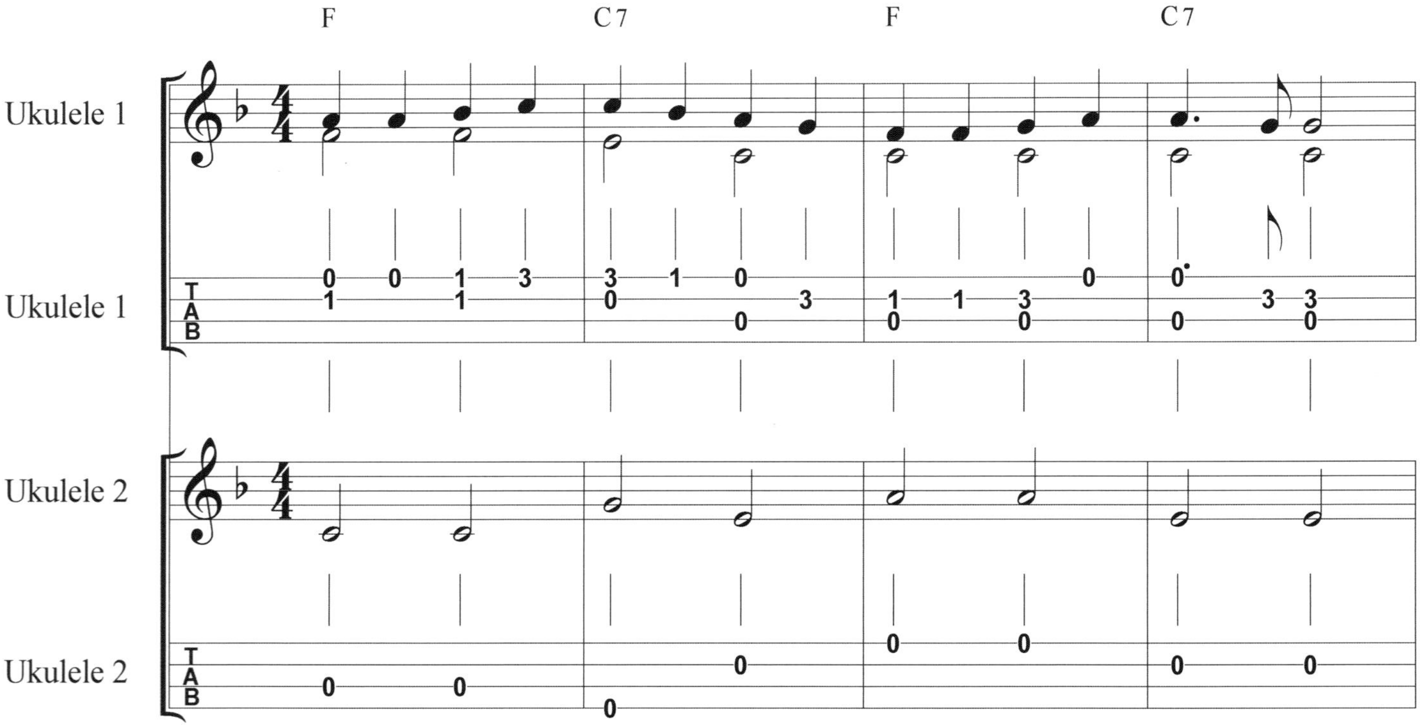

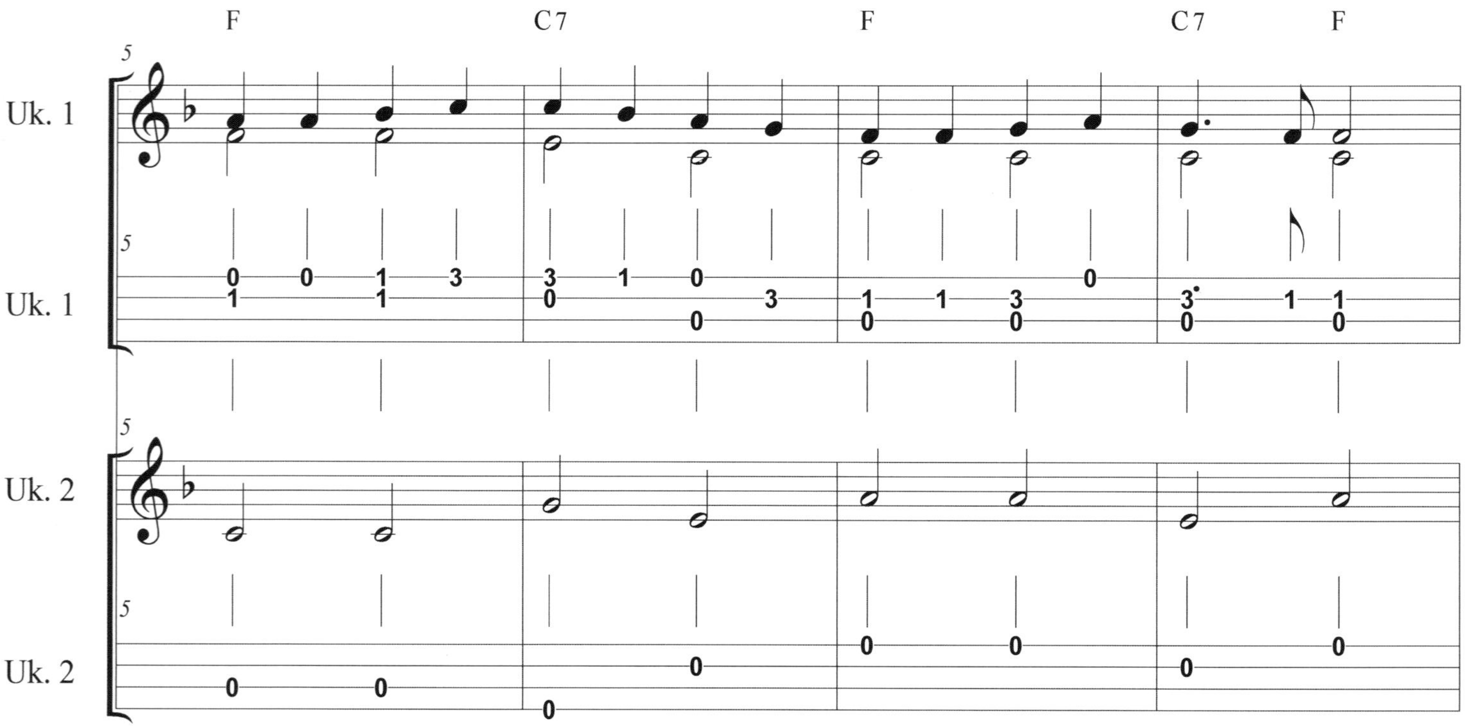

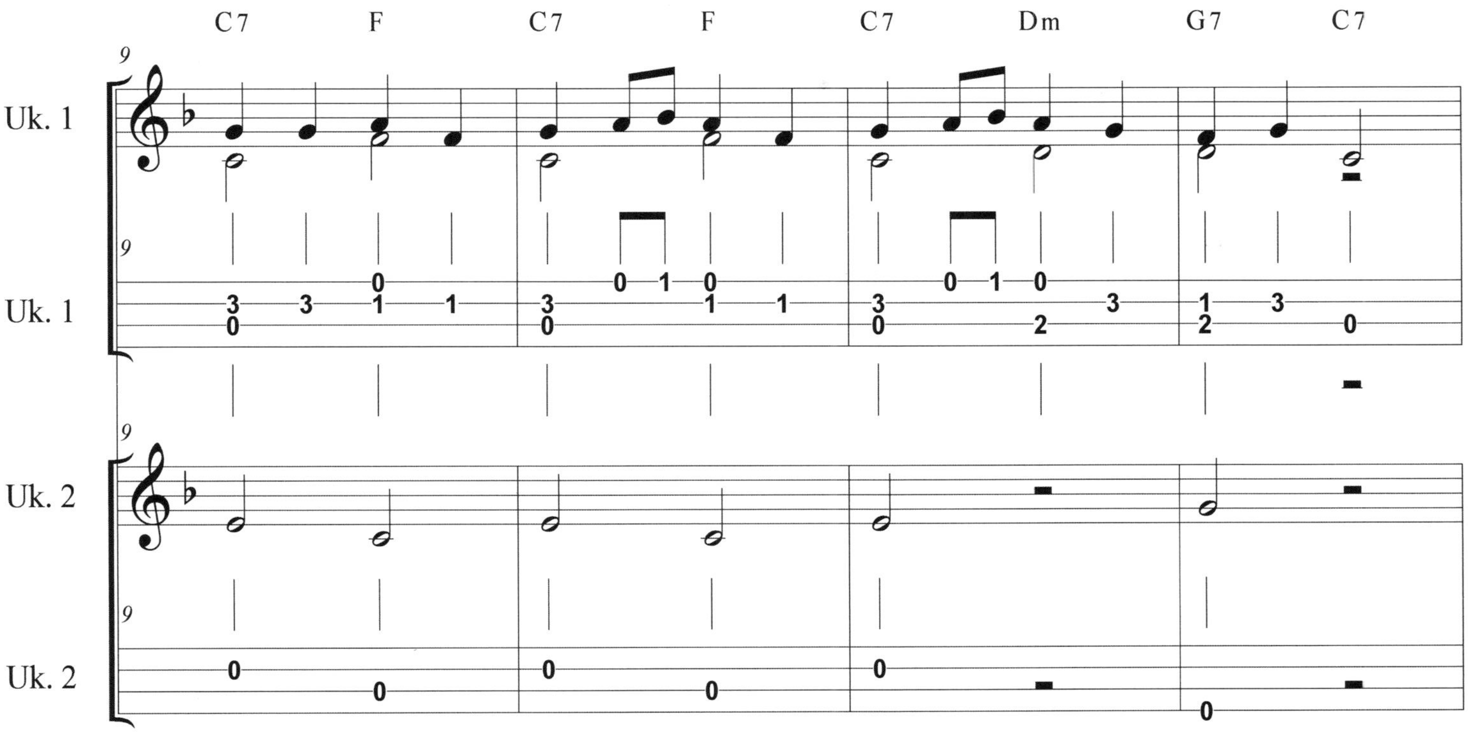
C7 F C7 F C7 Dm G7 C7
Uk. 1
Uk. 1
Uk. 2
Uk. 2

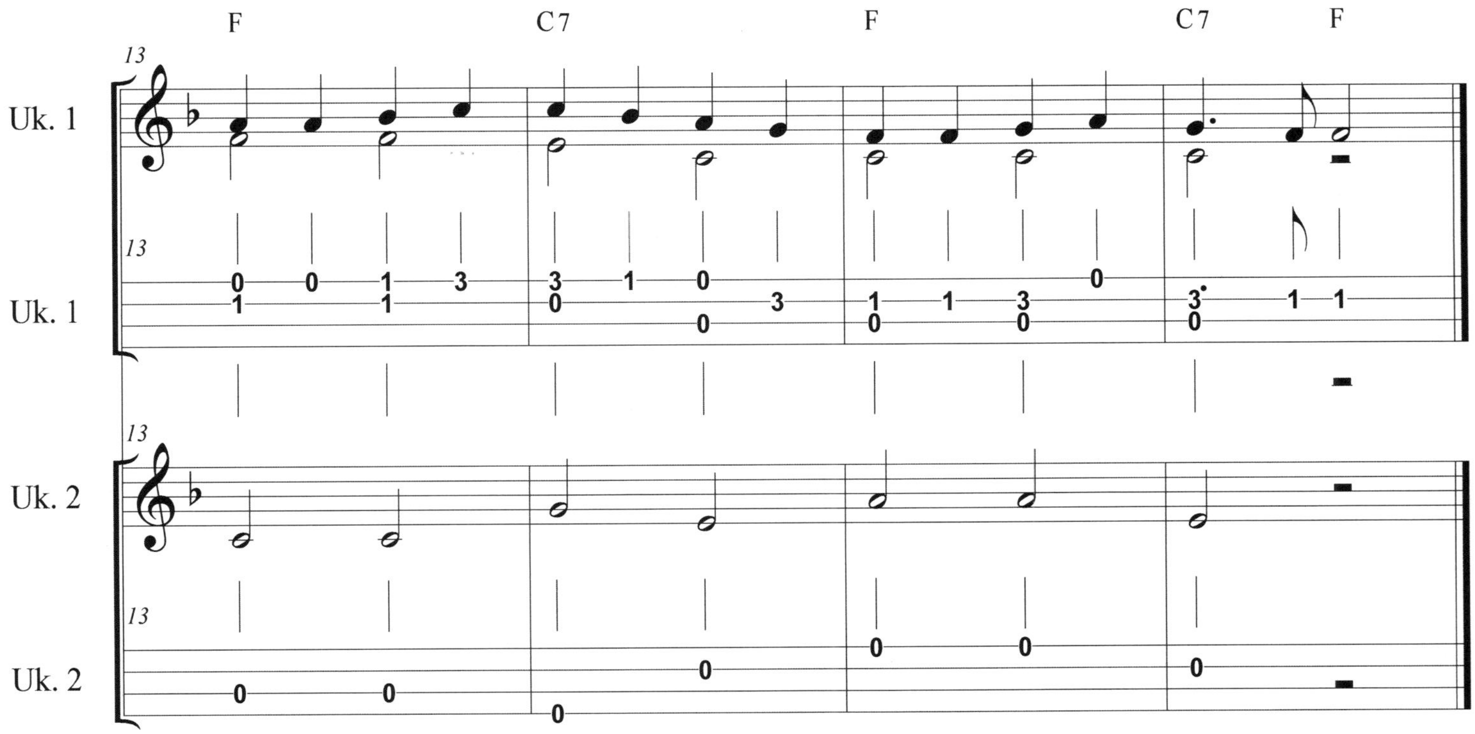
F C7 F C7 F
Uk. 1
Uk. 1
Uk. 2
Uk. 2

Oh! Susanna

Music: Stephen Foster (1826-1864)

arr: Ondřej Šárek

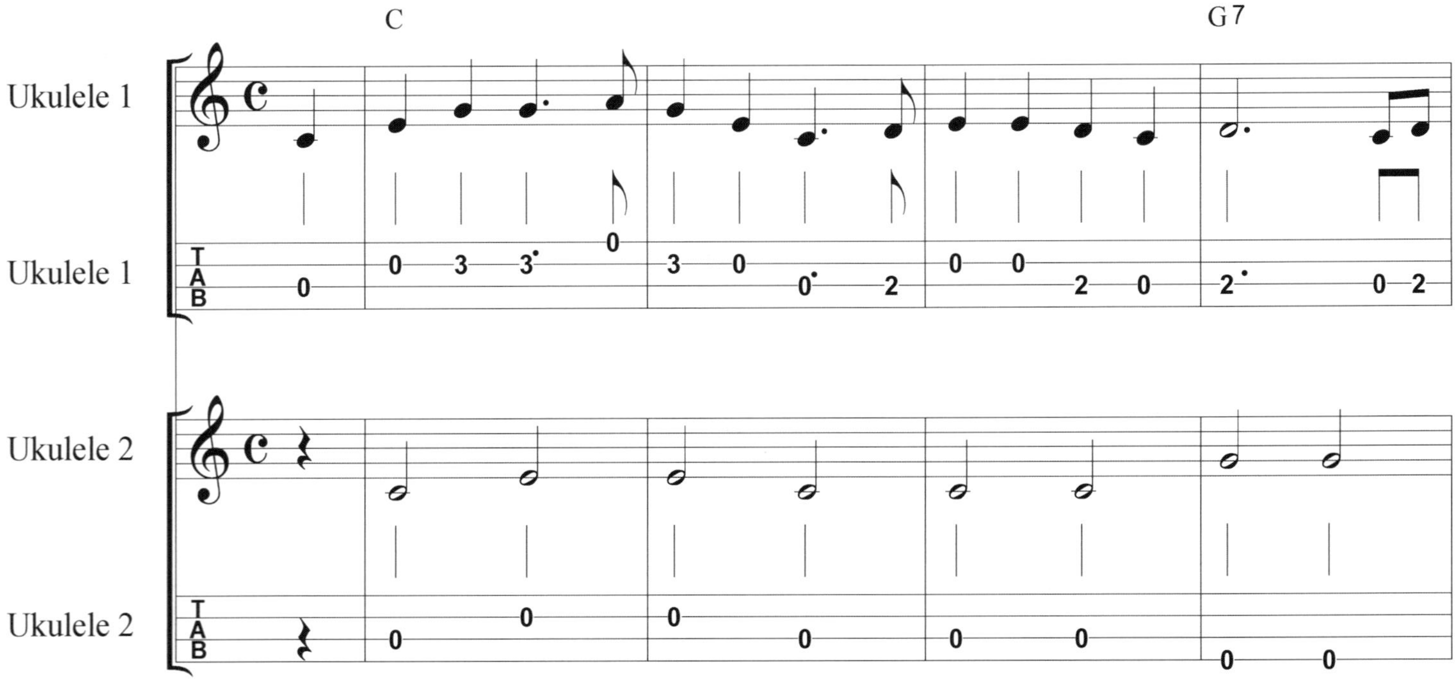

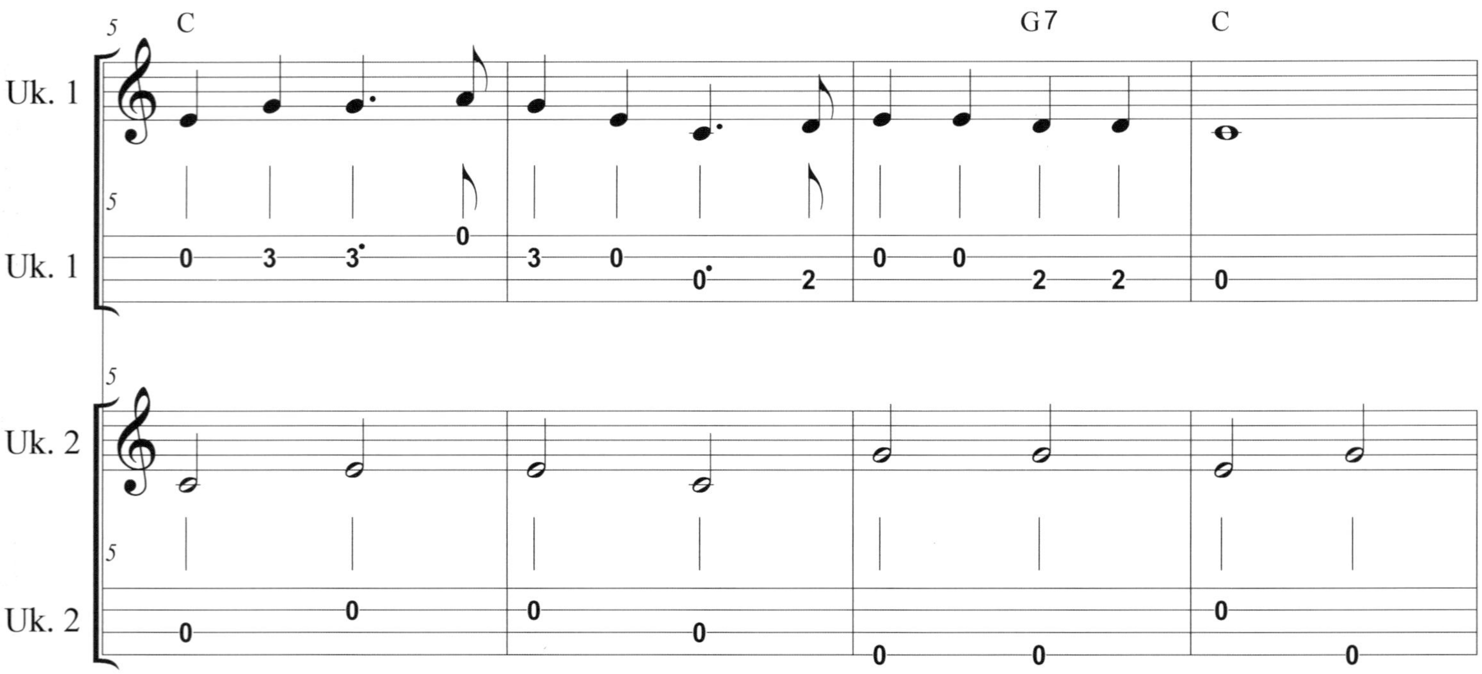

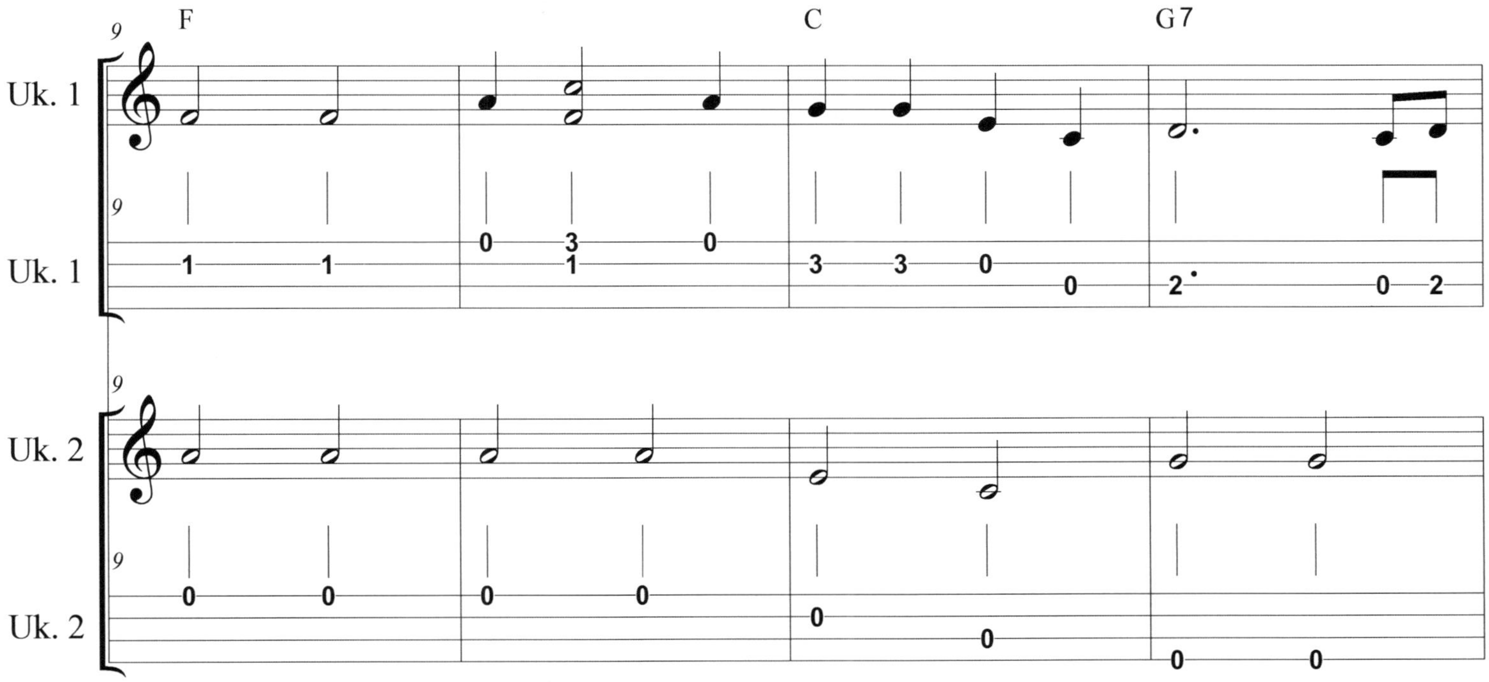
9
F
C
G7
Uk. 1
Uk. 1
Uk. 2
Uk. 2

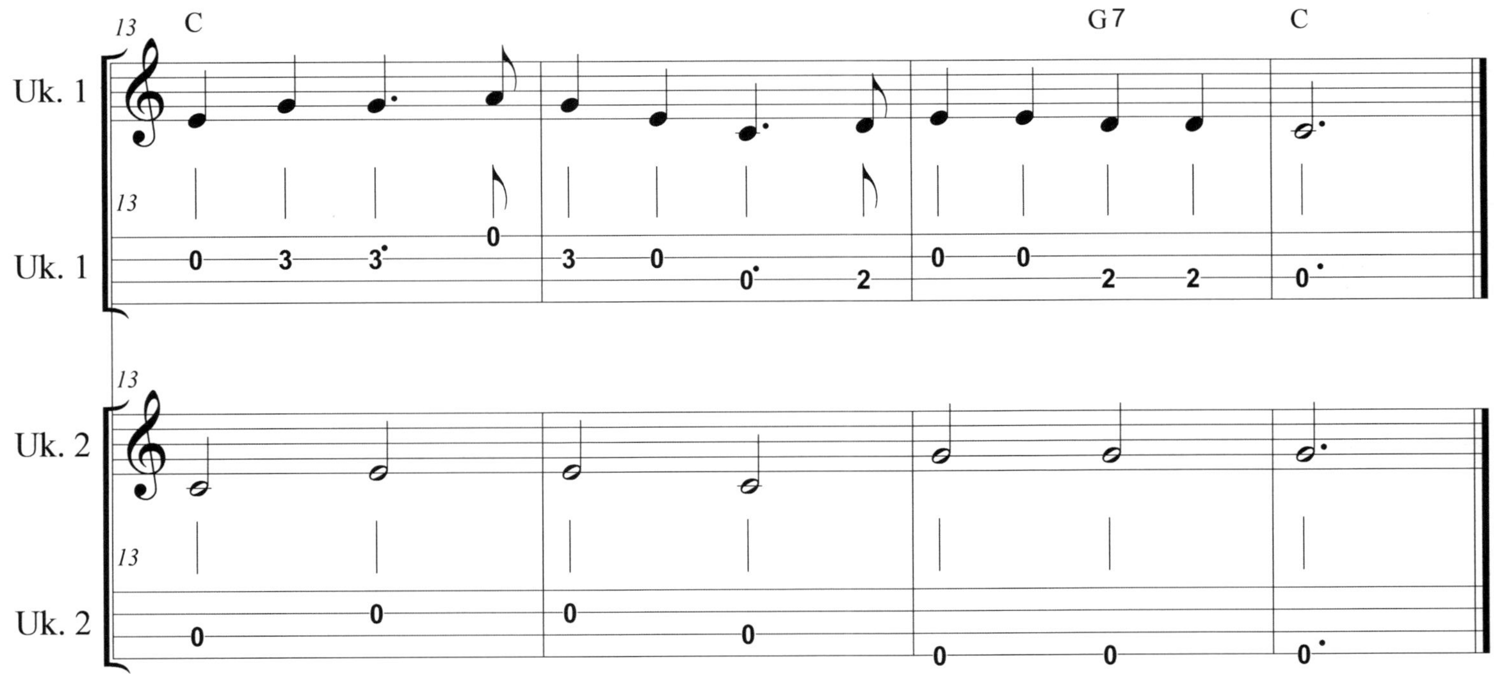
13
C
G7
C
Uk. 1
Uk. 1
Uk. 2
Uk. 2

On Top of Old Smokey

American folk song
arr: Ondřej Šárek

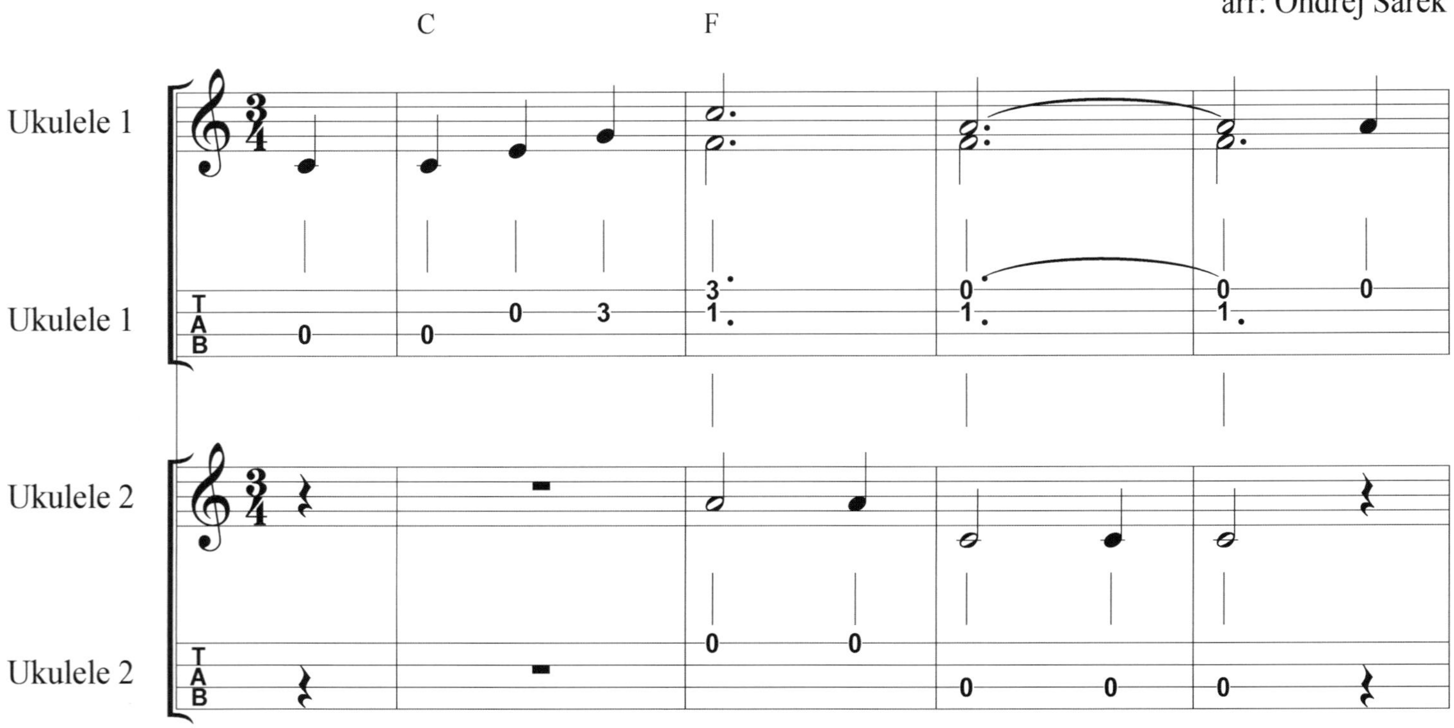

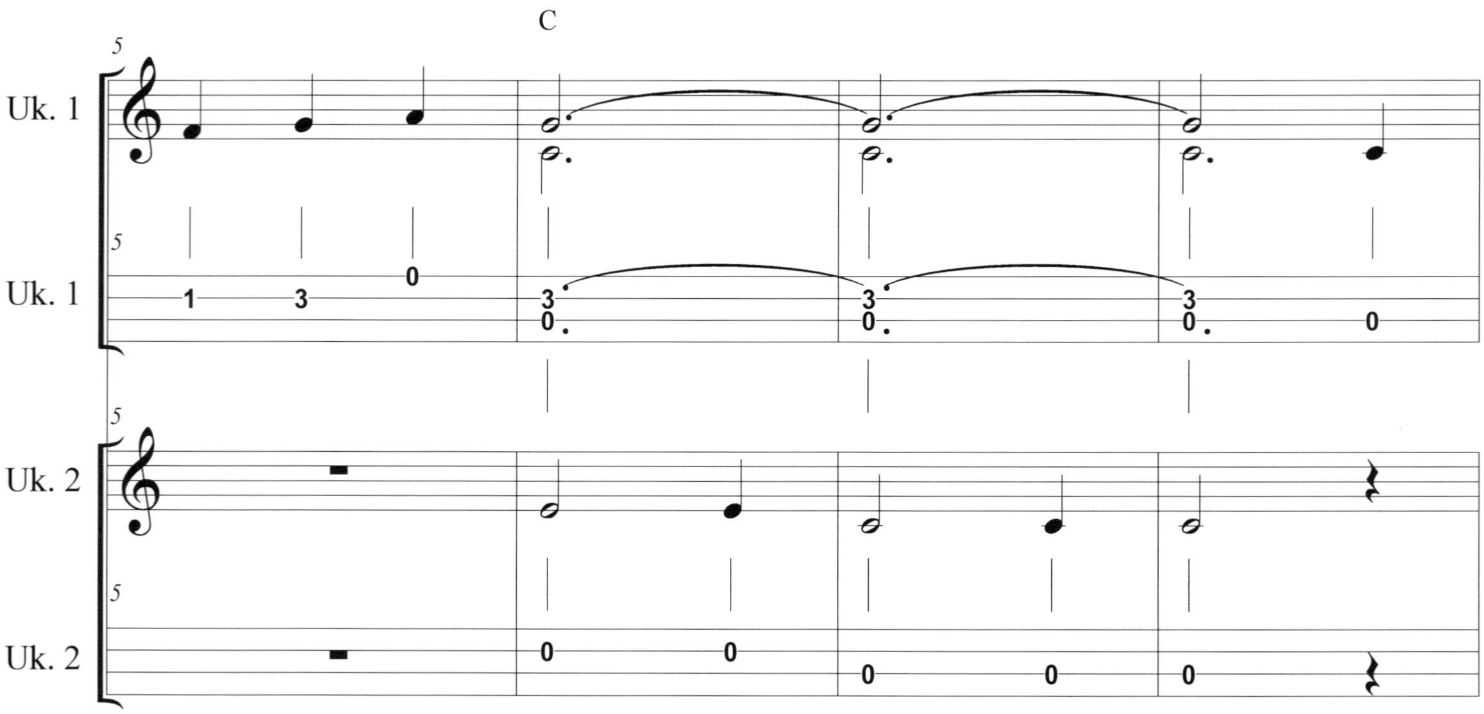

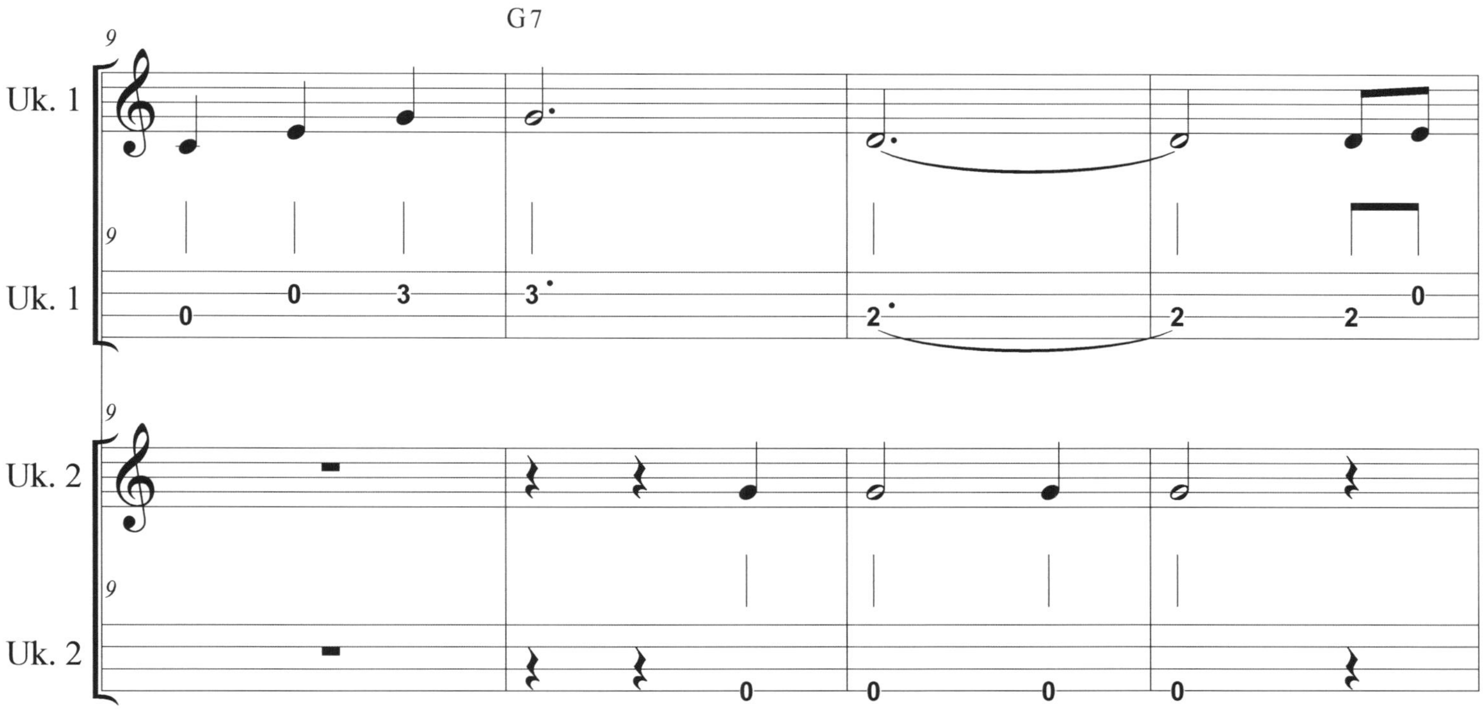
G7
9
Uk. 1
Uk. 1
Uk. 2
Uk. 2

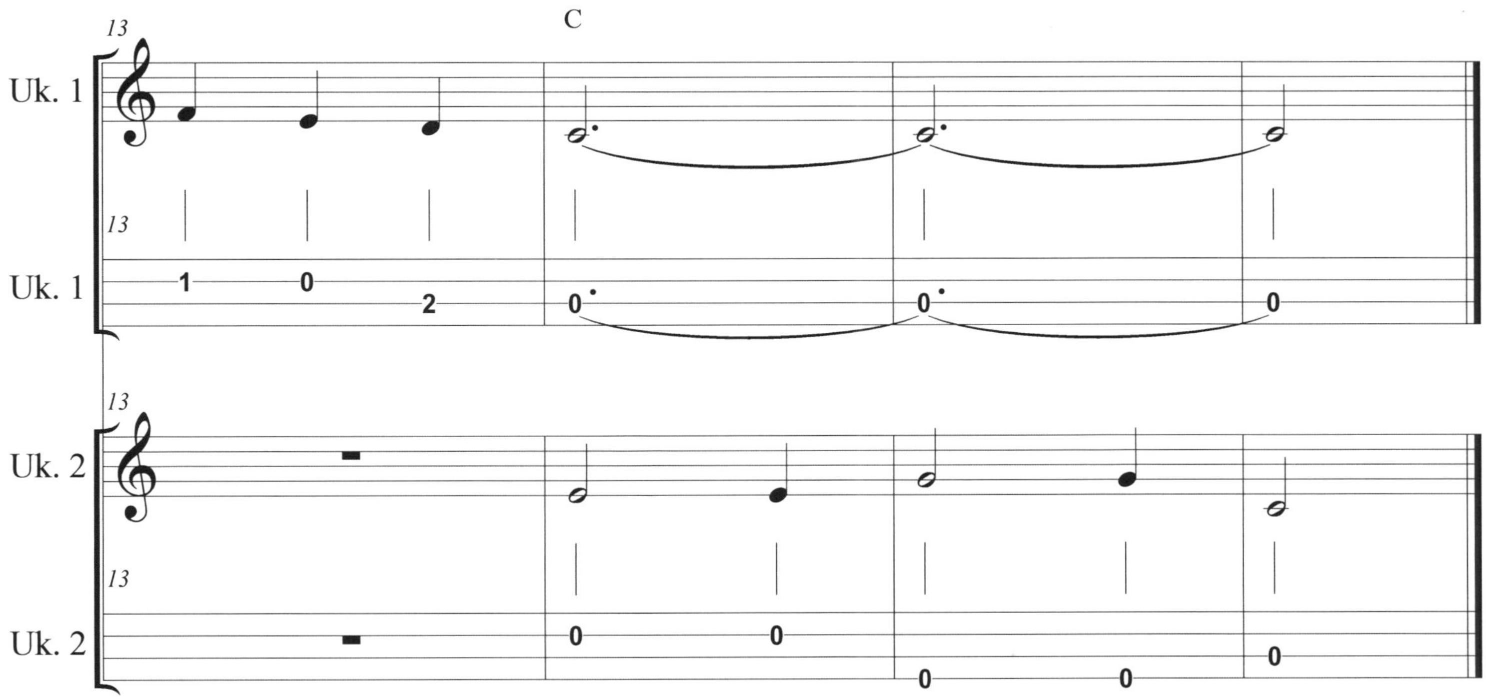
C
13
Uk. 1
Uk. 1
Uk. 2
Uk. 2

Roll In My Sweet Baby's Arms

American folk song
arr: Ondřej Šárek

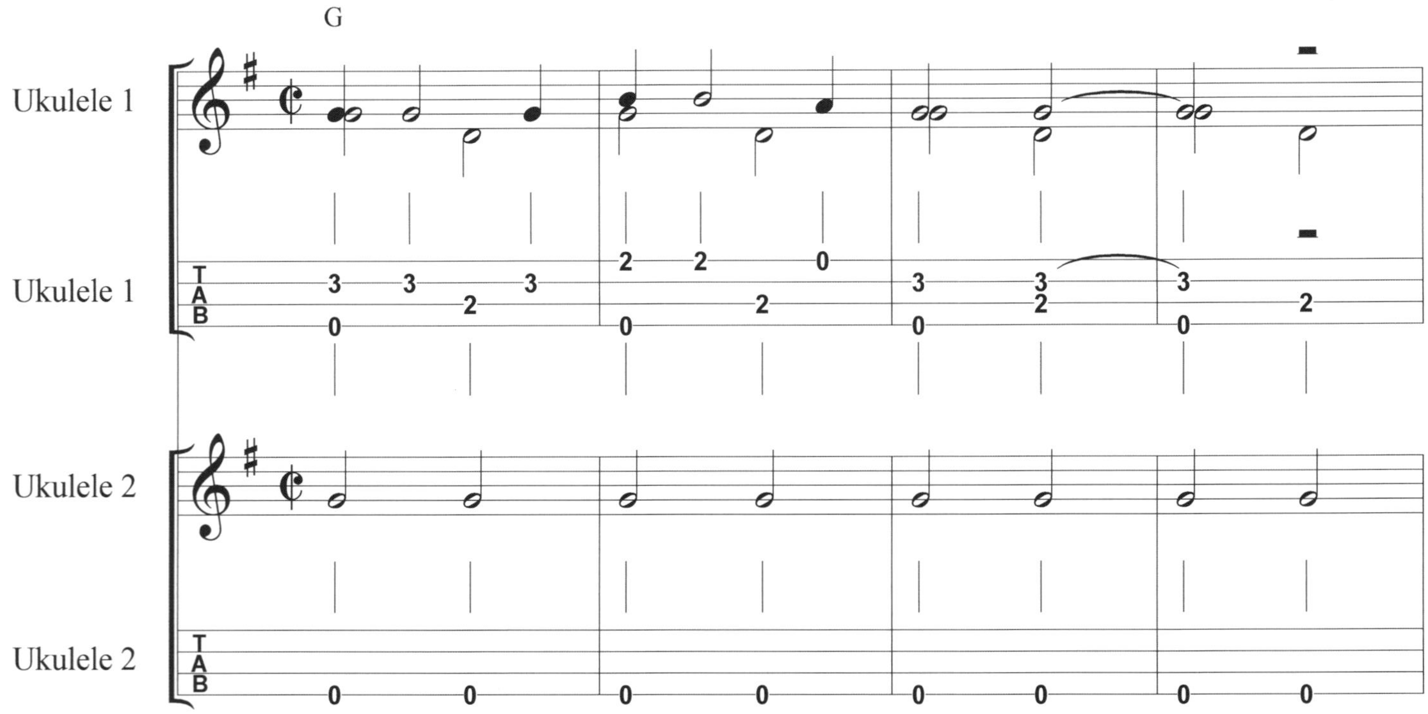

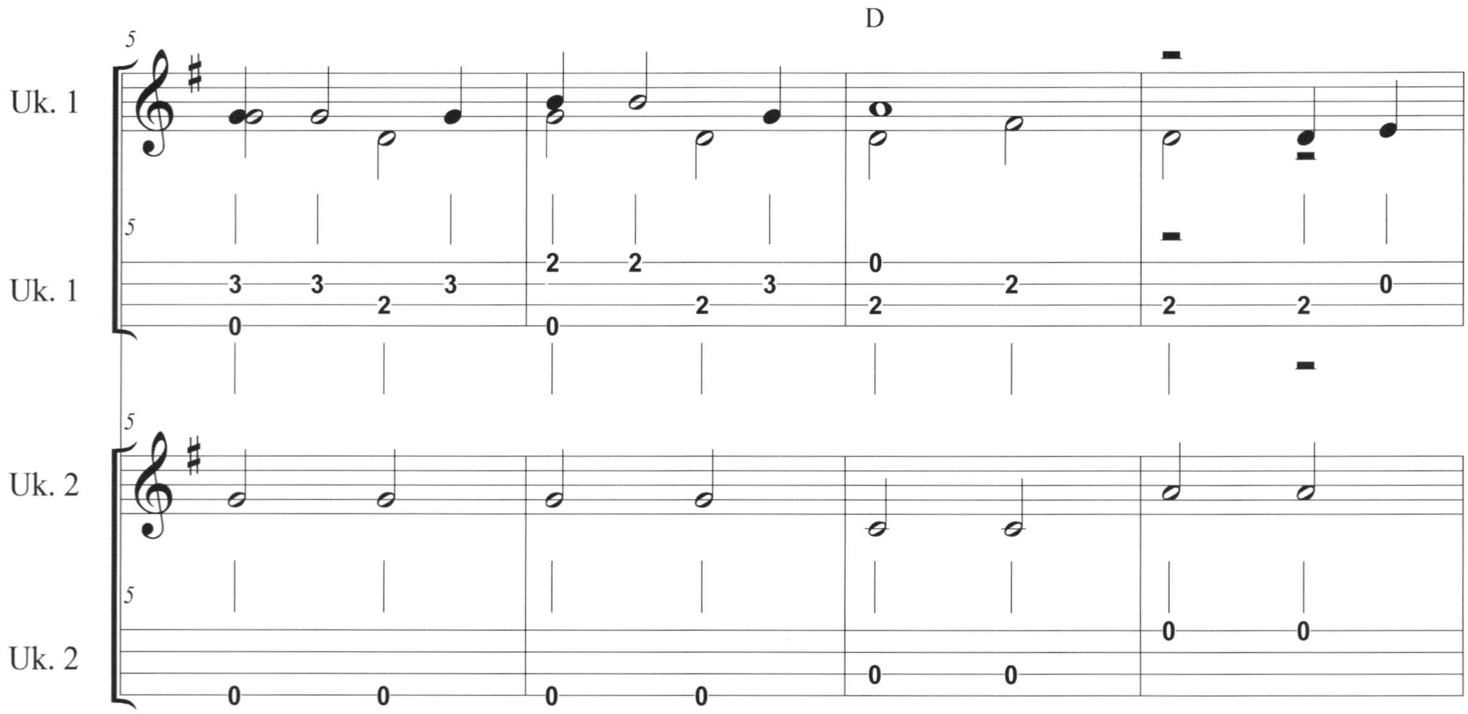

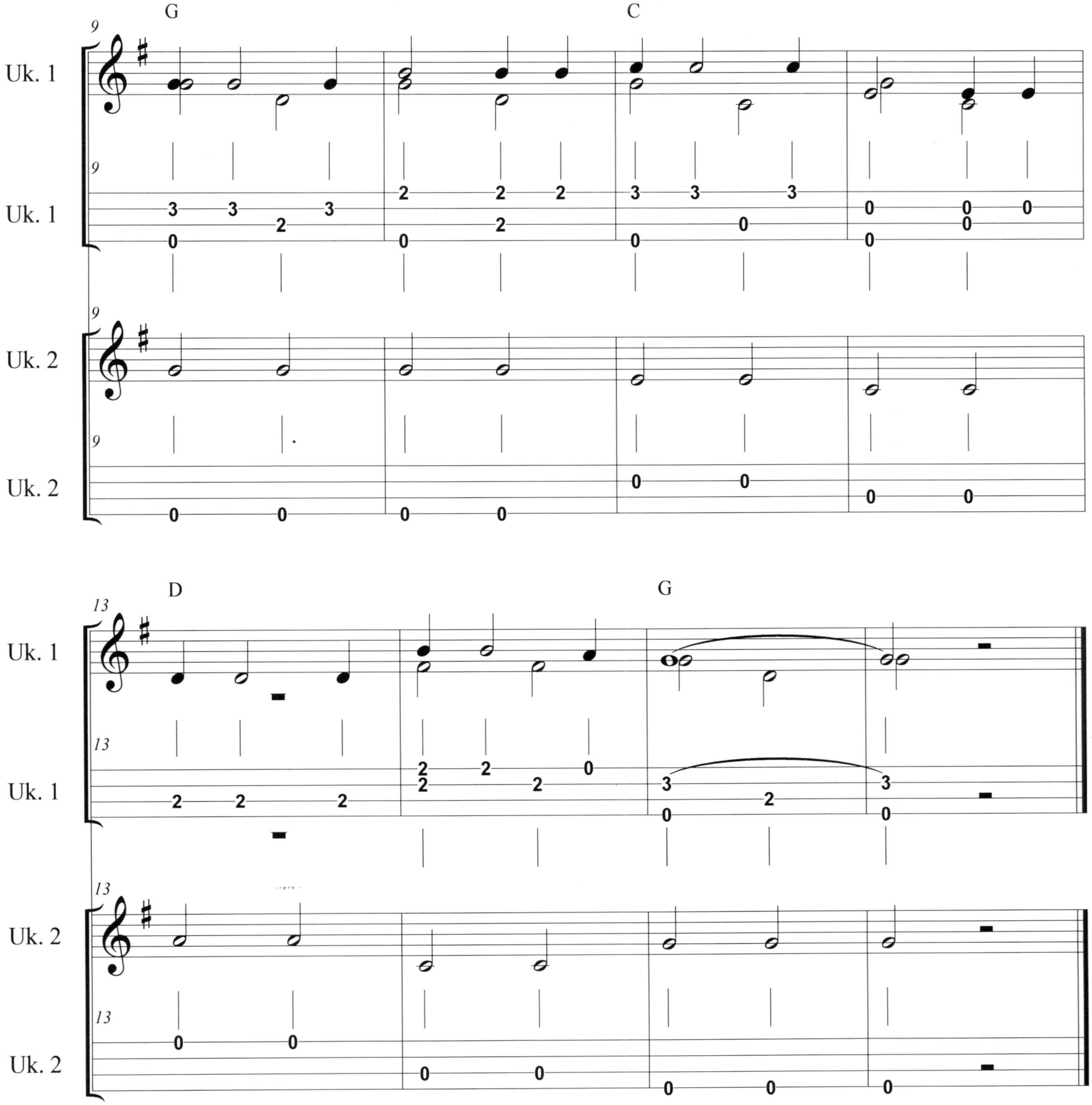
G
C
Uk. 1
Uk. 1
Uk. 2
Uk. 2
D
G
Uk. 1
Uk. 1
Uk. 2
Uk. 2

Salty Dog Blues

American Old-Time
arr: Ondřej Šárek

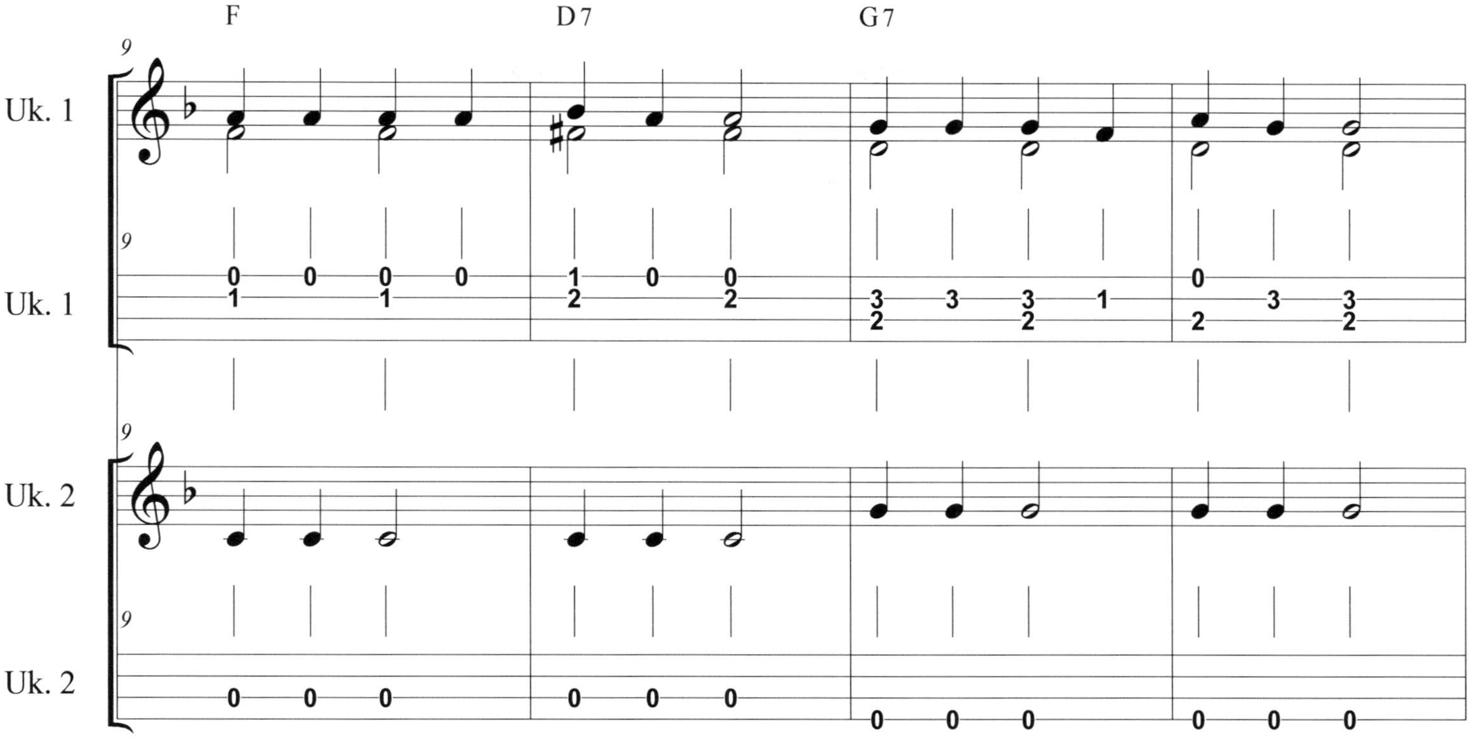
F
D7
G7
Uk. 1
Uk. 1
Uk. 2
Uk. 2

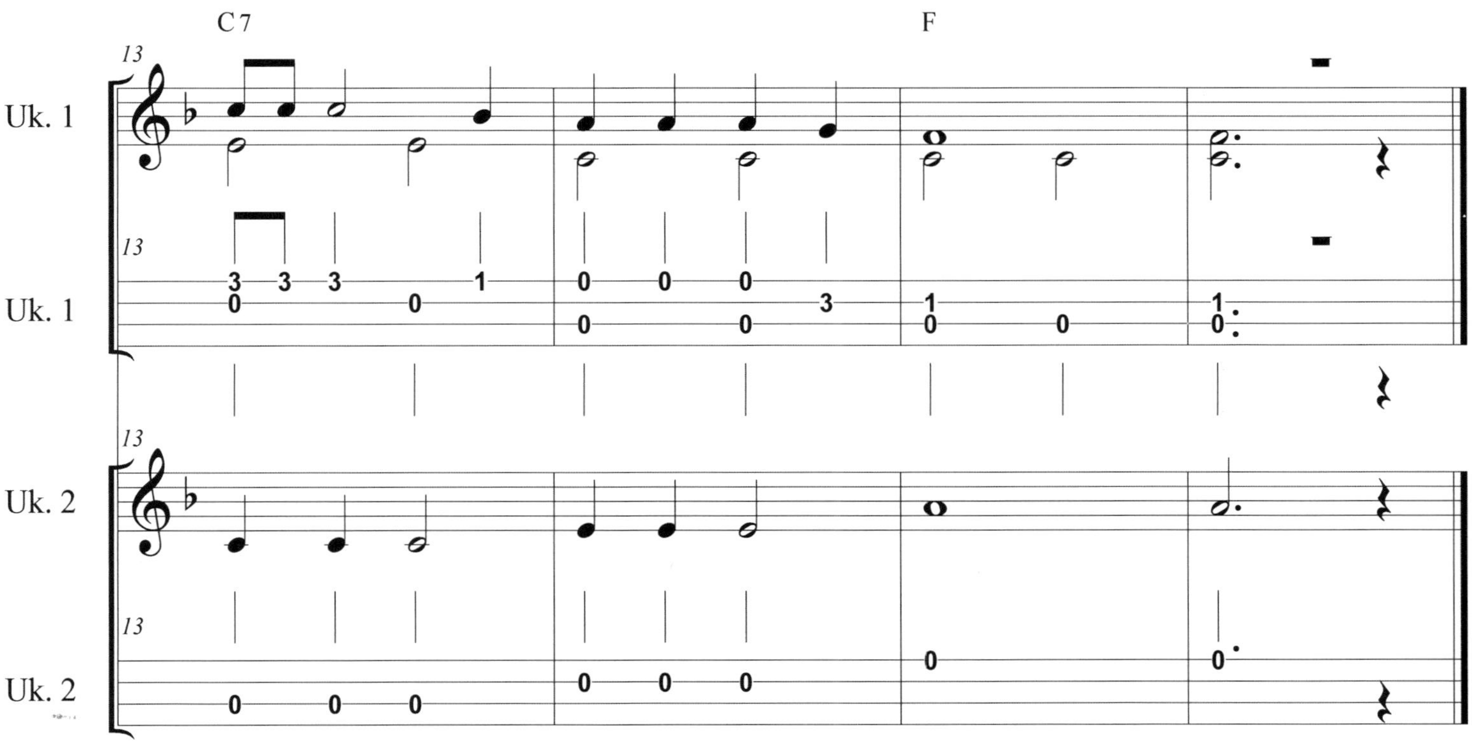
C7
F
Uk. 1
Uk. 1
Uk. 2
Uk. 2

The First Noel

English carol
arr: Ondřej Šárek

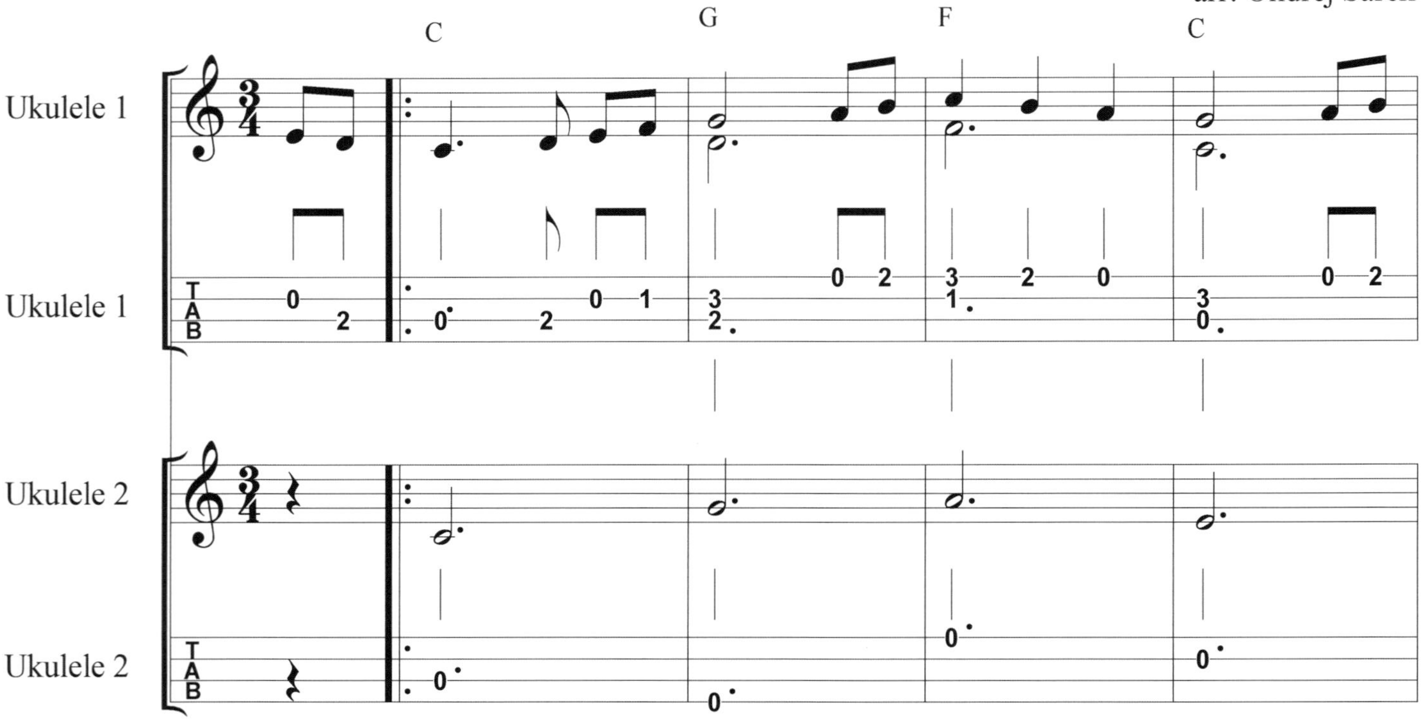

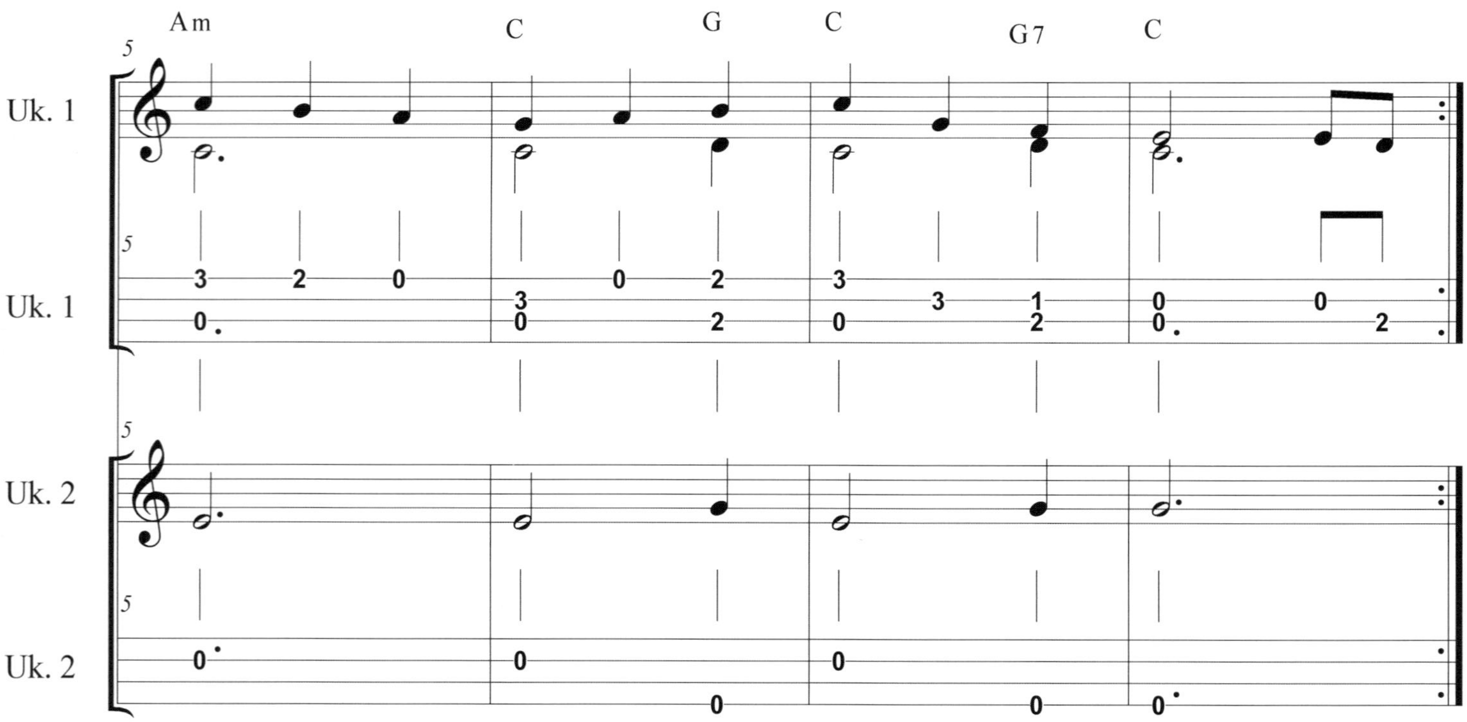

9
C G F C
Uk. 1
Uk. 1
Uk. 2
Uk. 2

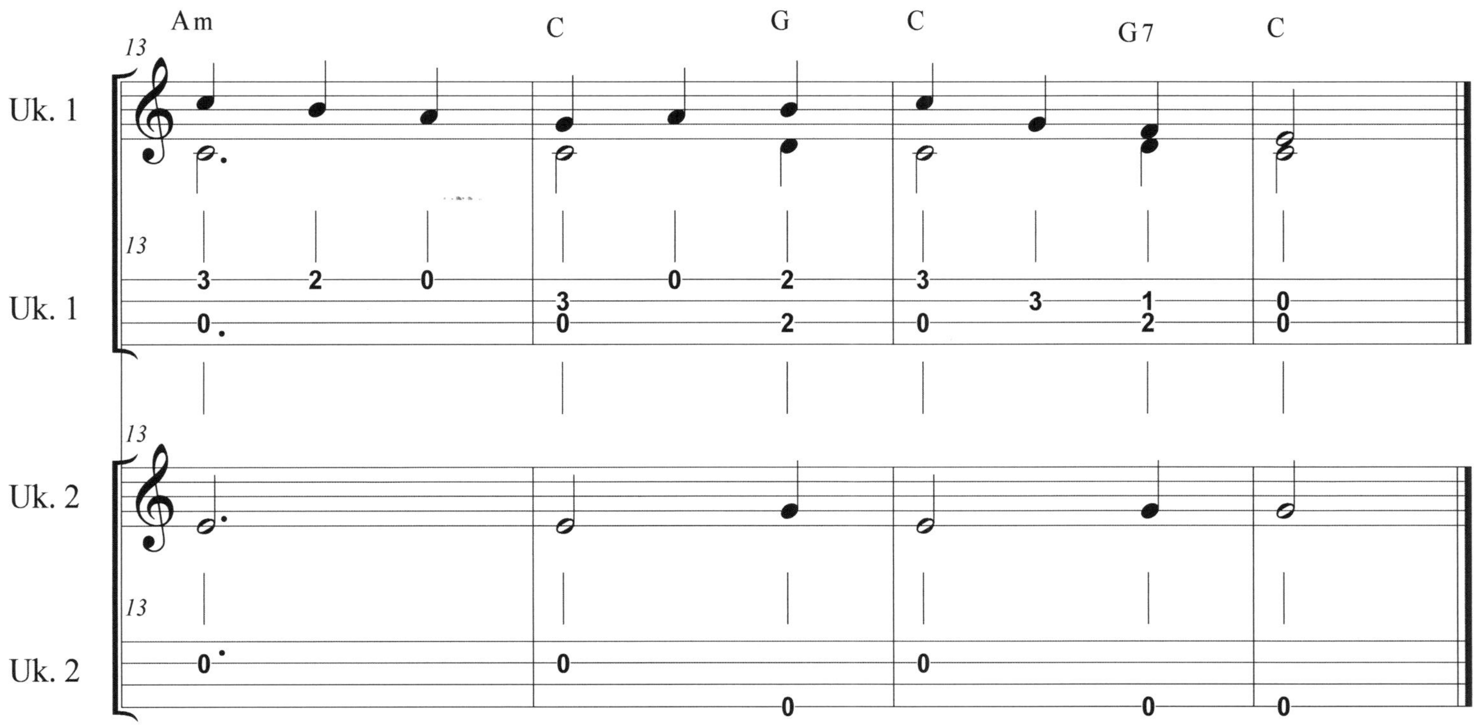
13
Am C G C G7 C
Uk. 1
Uk. 1
Uk. 2
Uk. 2

The Street of Laredo

American folk song
arr: Ondřej Šárek

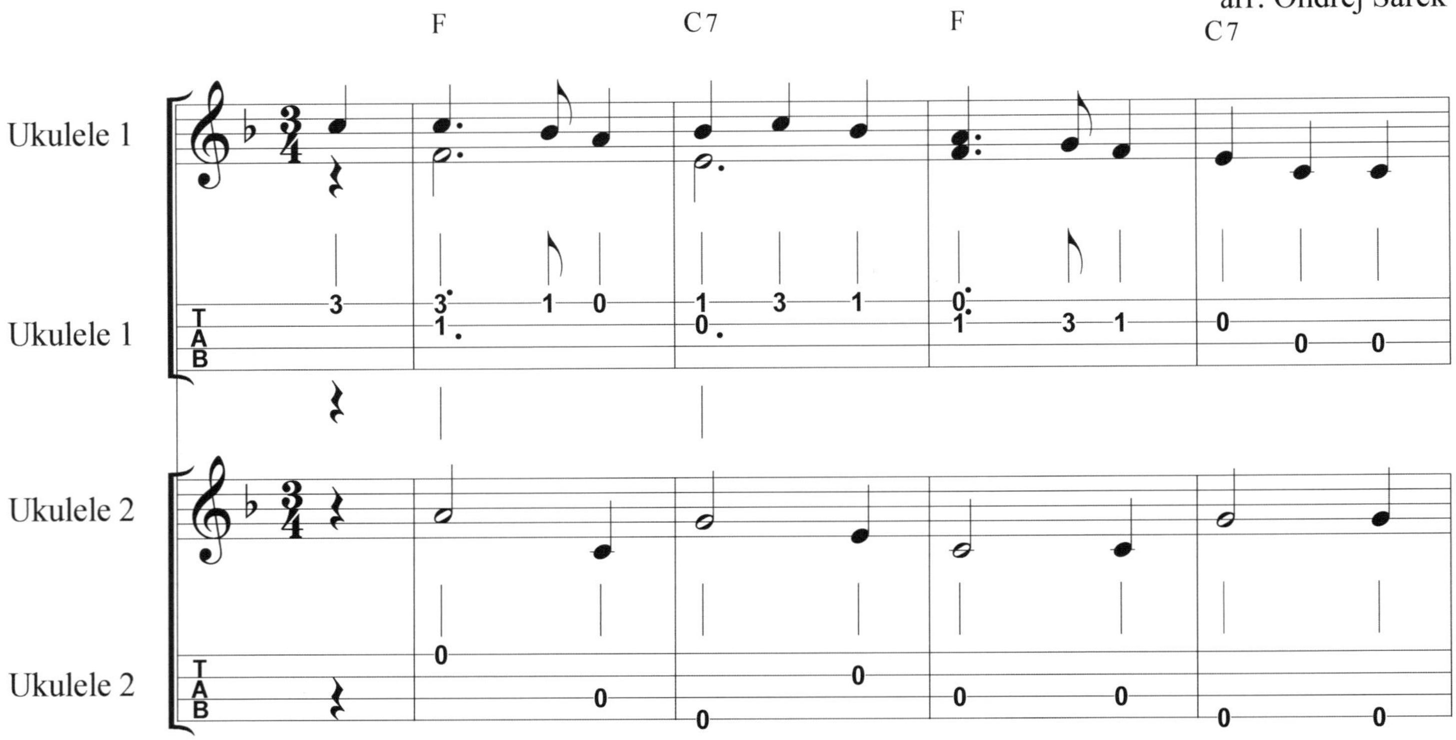

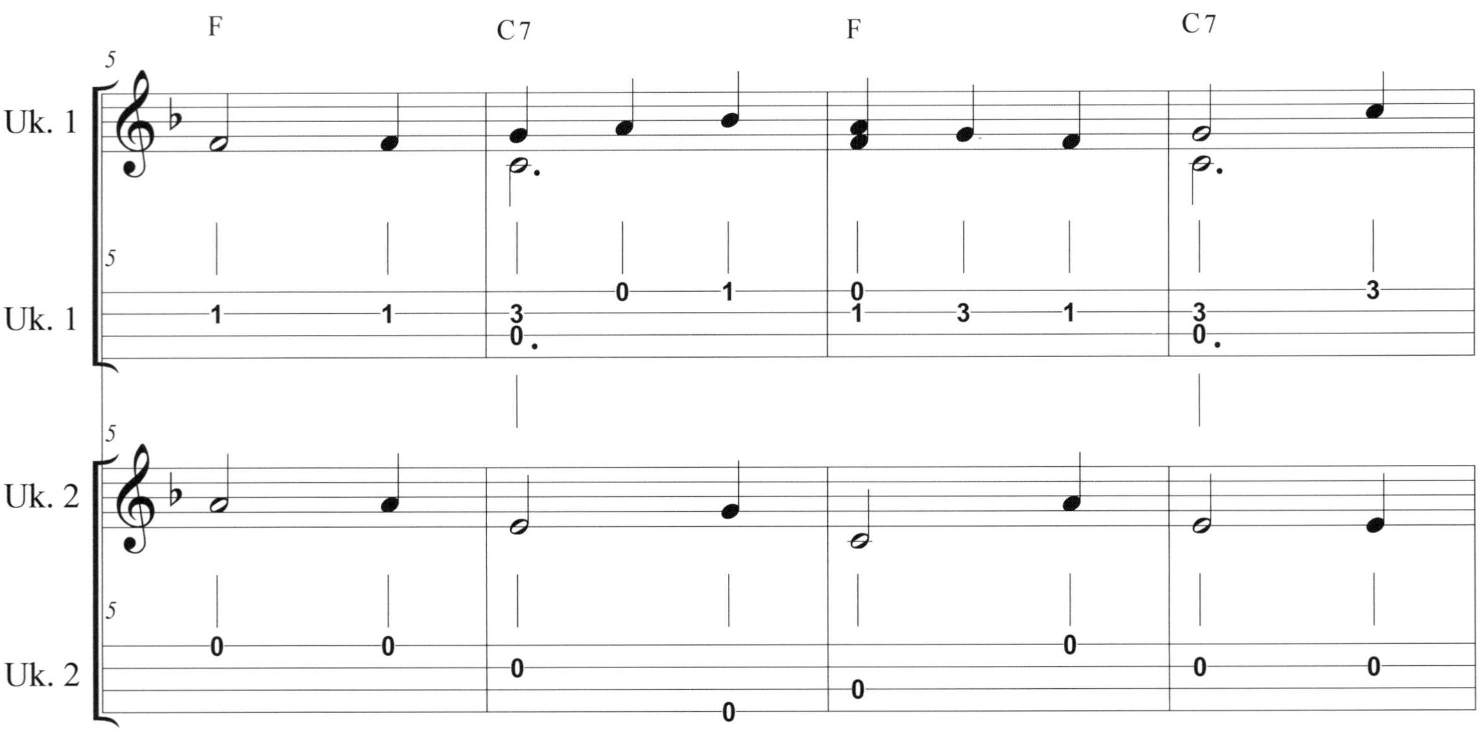

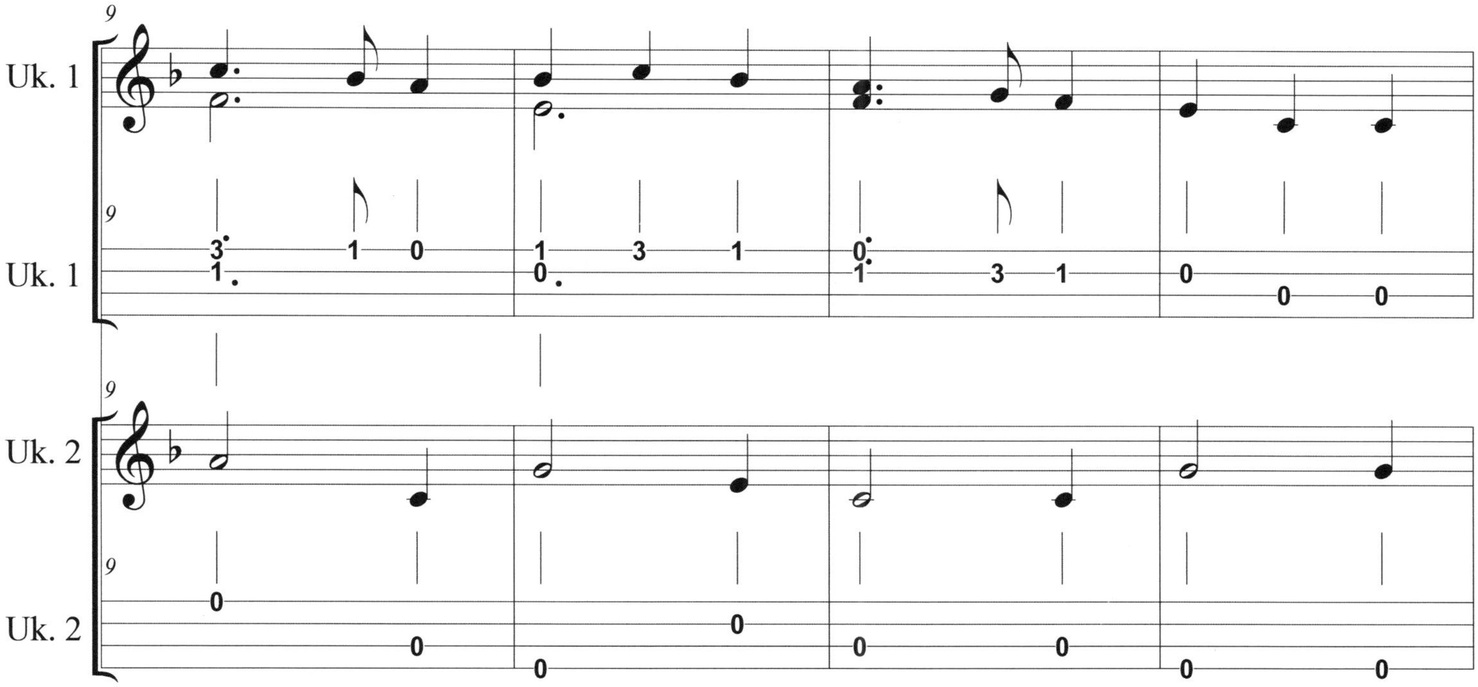
Uk. 1
Uk. 1
Uk. 2
Uk. 2

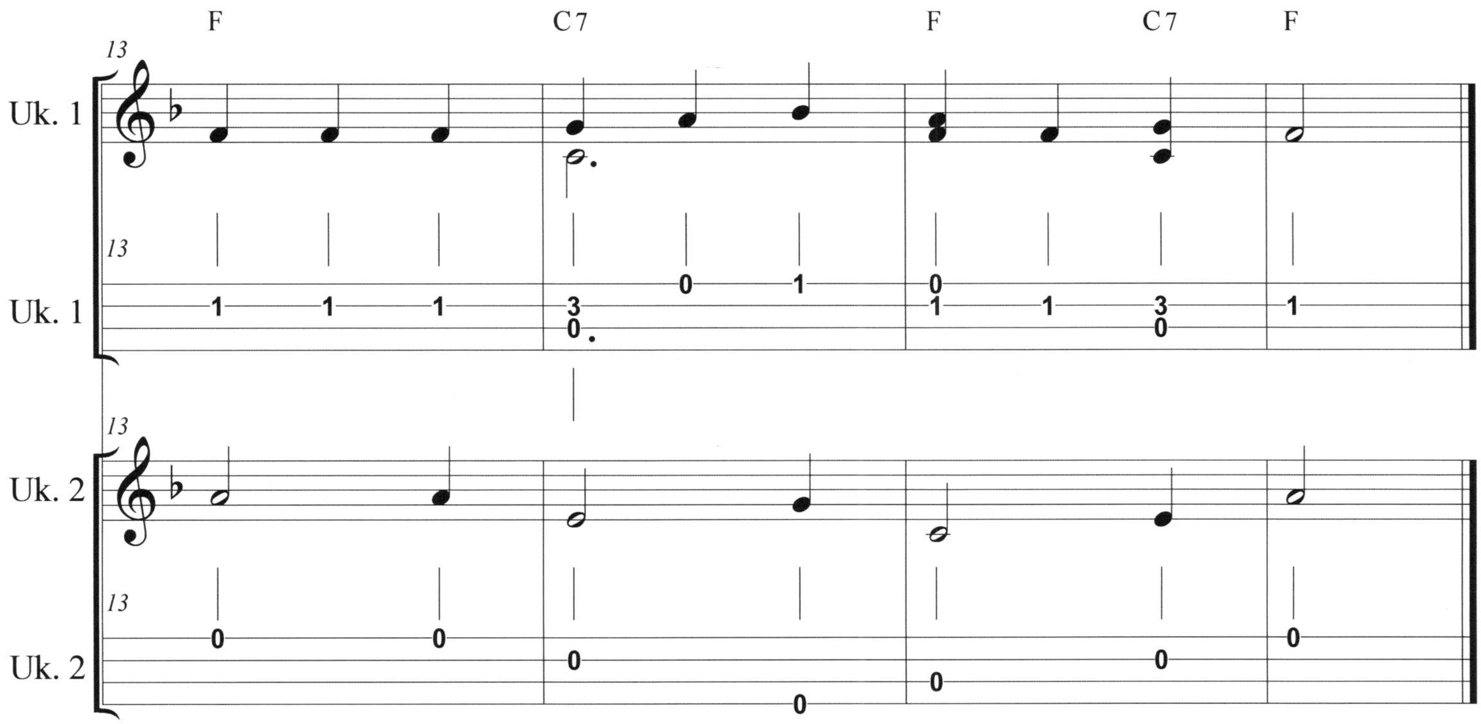
F
C 7
F
C 7
F
Uk. 1
Uk. 1
Uk. 2
Uk. 2

Twinkle, Twinkle Little Star

French folk song
arr: Ondřej Šárek

D
A7
D
G
Uk. 1
Uk. 1
Uk. 2
Uk. 2
D
G
D
A7
D
Uk. 1
Uk. 1
Uk. 2
Uk. 2

The Water Is Wide

English Ballad
arr: Ondřej Šárek

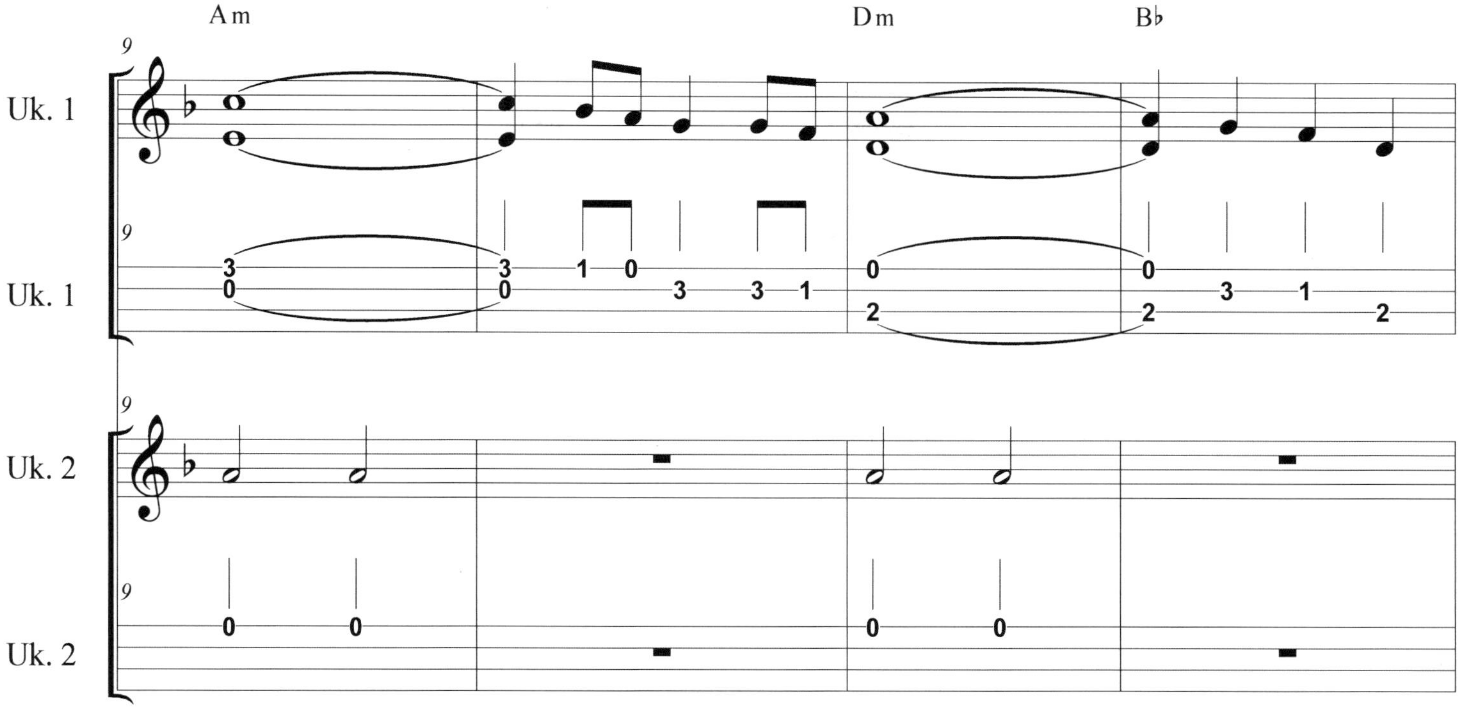
Am
Dm
B♭
9
Uk. 1
Uk. 1
Uk. 2
Uk. 2

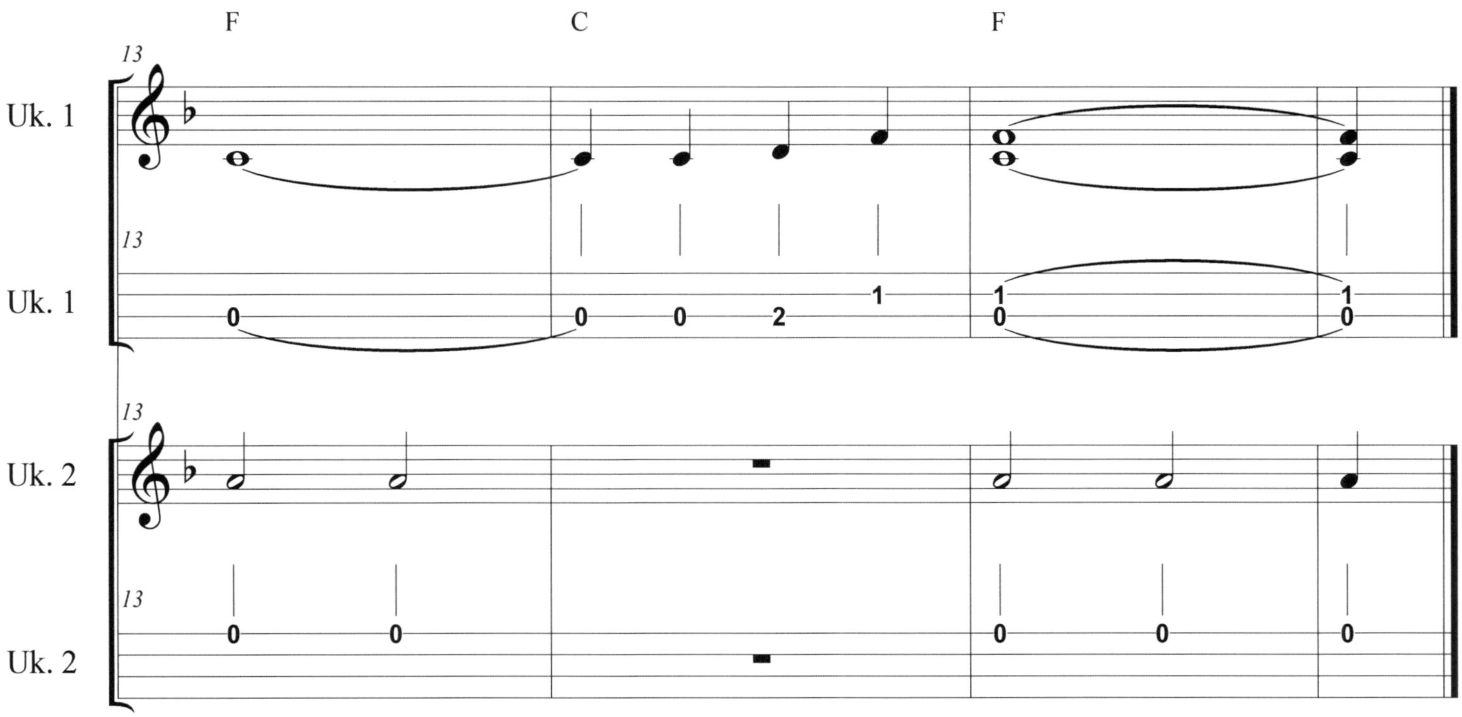
F
C
F
13
Uk. 1
Uk. 1
Uk. 2
Uk. 2

We Wish You a Merry Christmas

English carol
arr: Ondřej Šárek

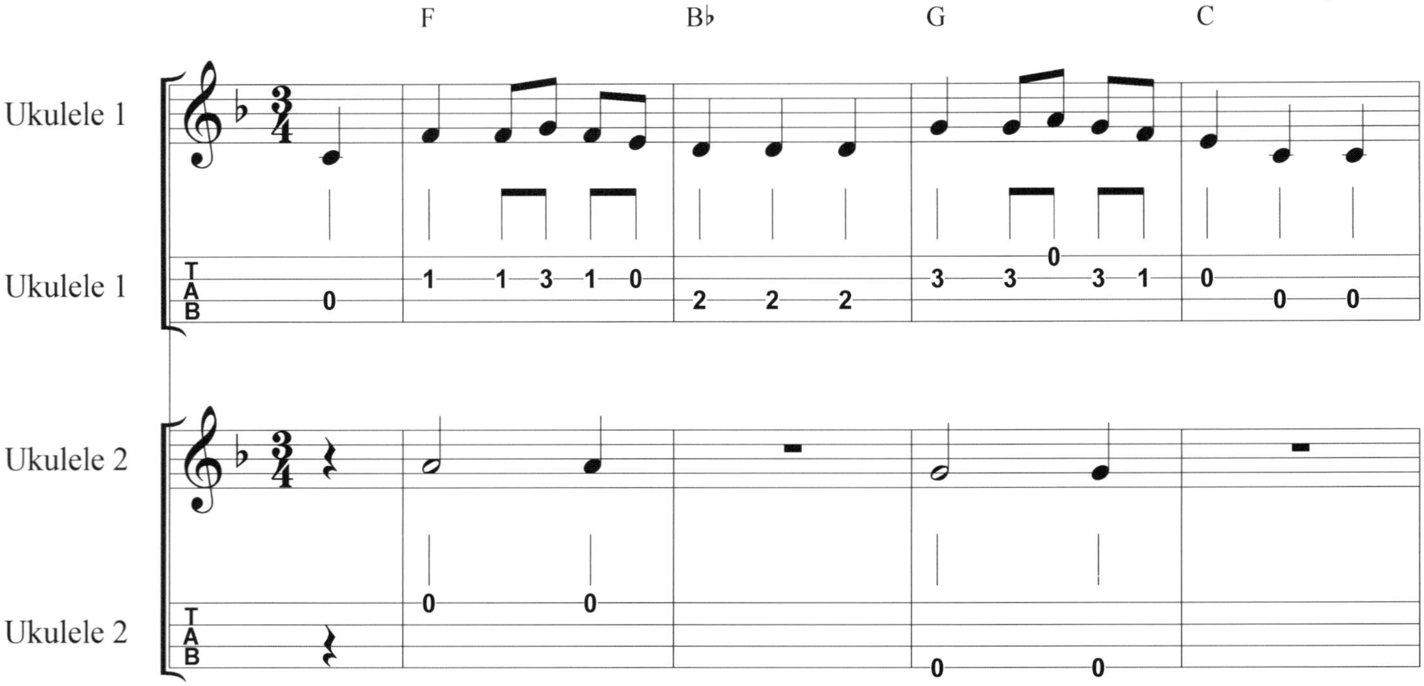

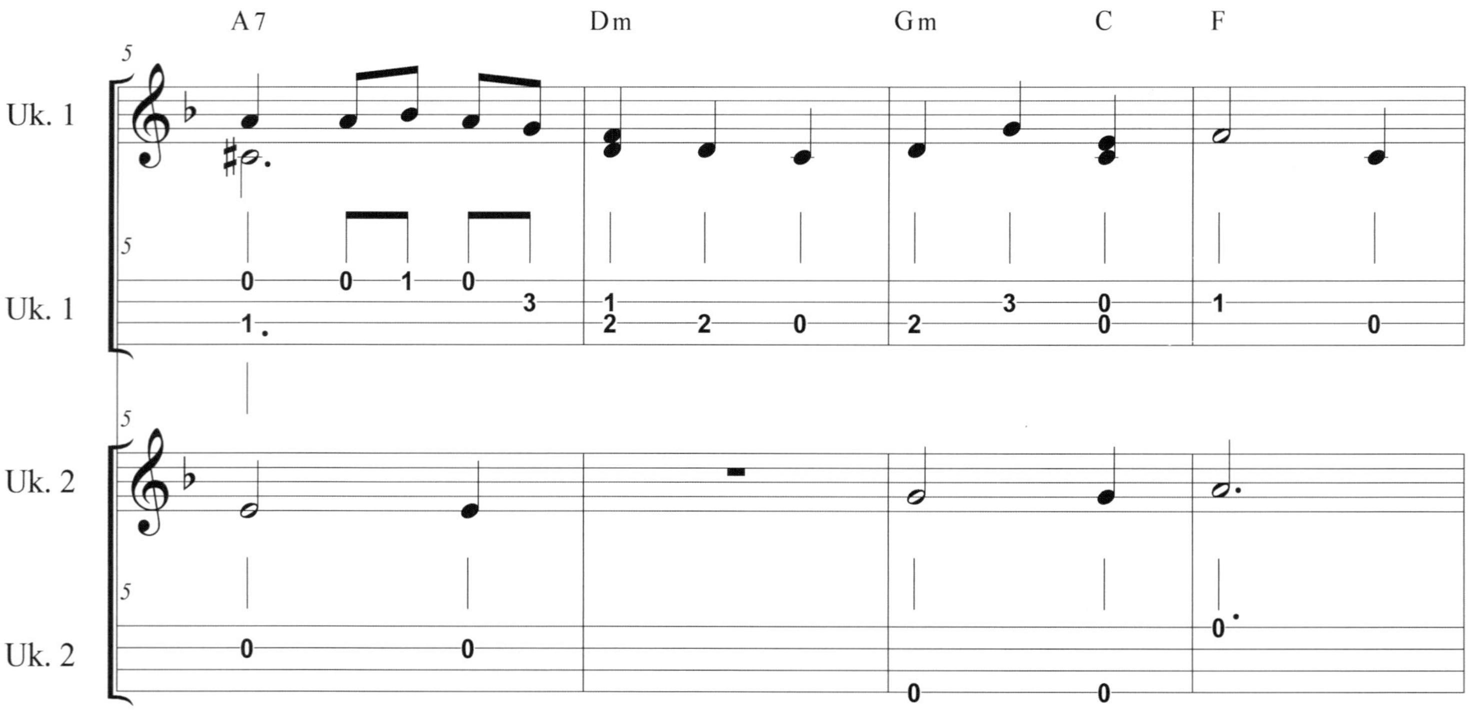

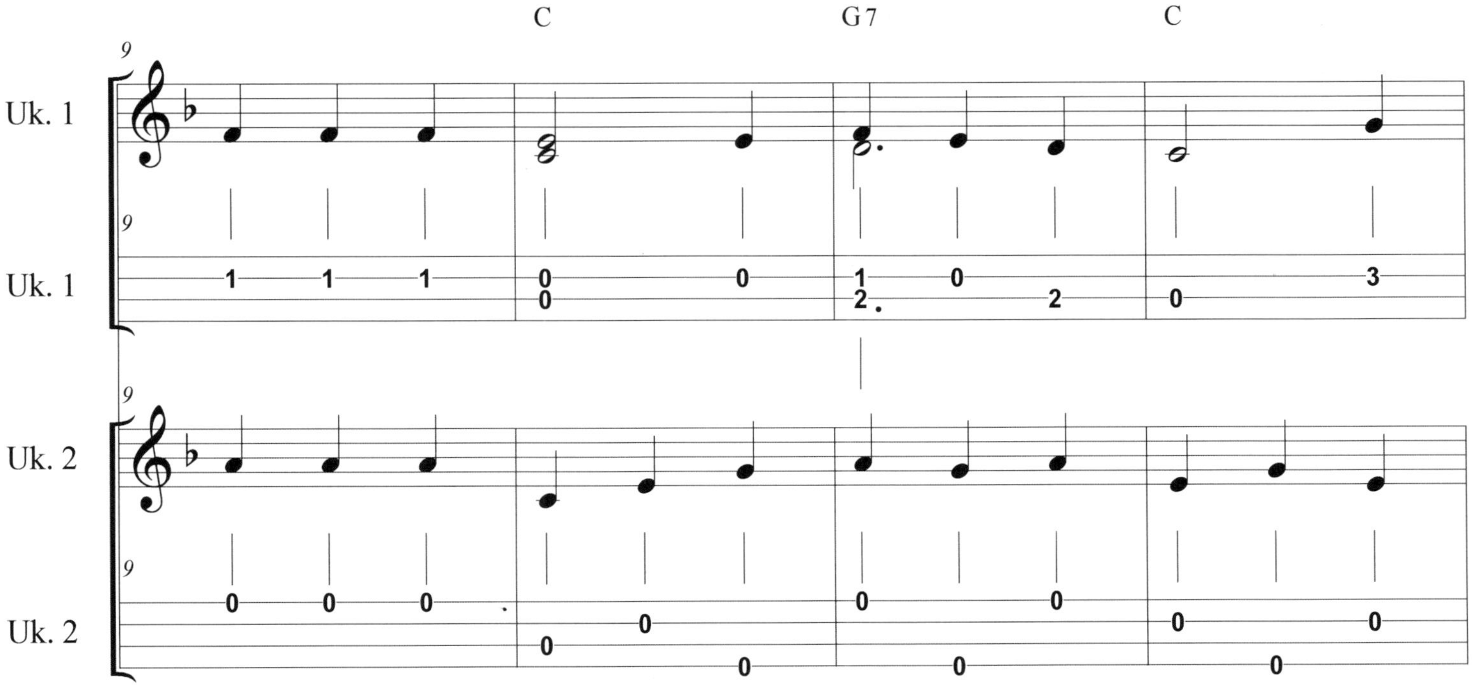
C
G7
C
Uk. 1
Uk. 1
Uk. 2
Uk. 2

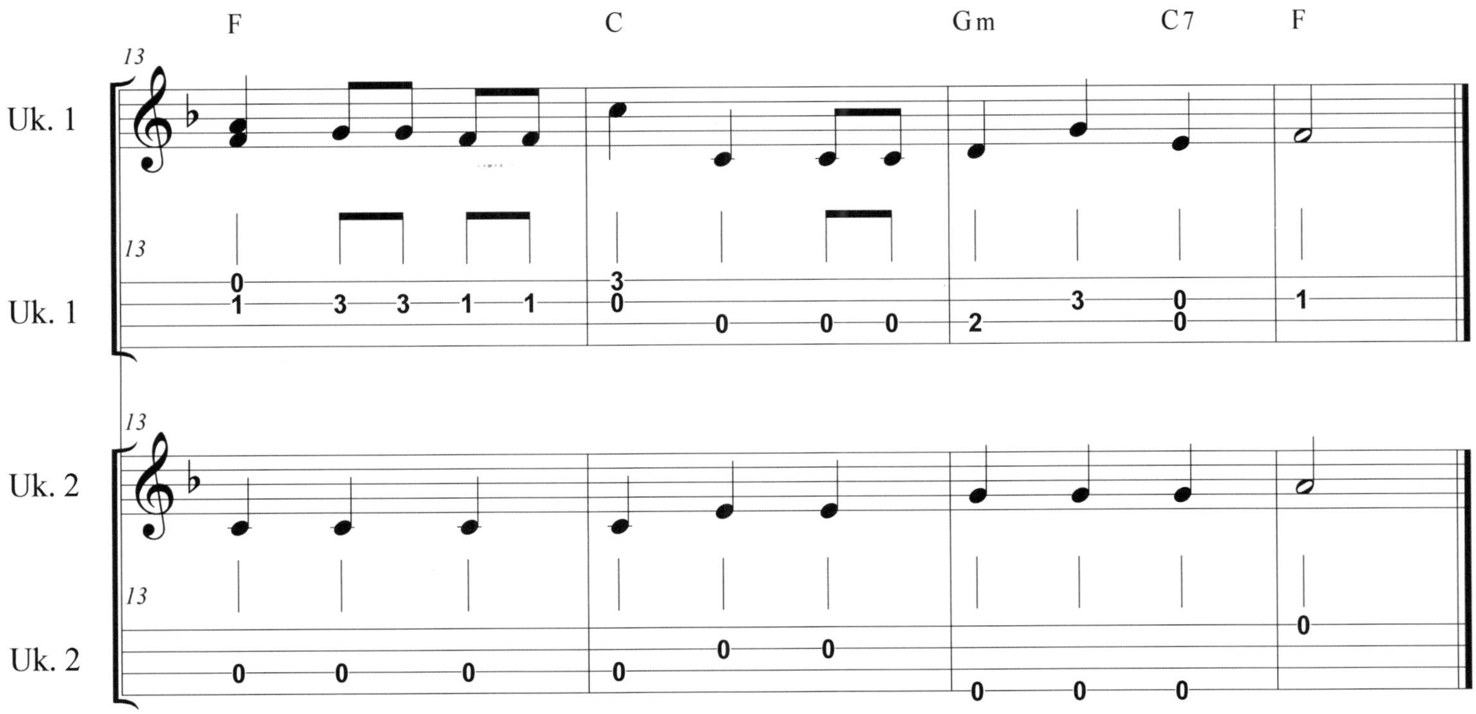
F
C
Gm
C7
F
Uk. 1
Uk. 1
Uk. 2
Uk. 2

Other Mel Bay Ukulele Books